out of the
VALLEY

To Bethan, Elen, Siôn and Gwenllian
for suffering my dramatic moments;
also Caitlin, Erin, Macsen and Lleu
for occasionally laughing at my jokes!

out of the
VALLEY

The Autobiography of a Media Man

Richard Lewis

Acknowledgements

Grateful thanks to Herbert Williams for his foreword 'putting it all in perspective'. To my son Siôn for his efforts with the computer! To Menna Richards, Director BBC Wales and Iona Jones, Chief Executive of S4C for permission to publish various publicity pictures of past productions. To Lefi Gruffudd of Y Lolfa publishers for his patience in entertaining the project!

First impression: 2010
© Richard Lewis & Y Lolfa Cyf., 2010

Cover design: Alan Thomas

ISBN: 9781847711496

Printed on acid-free and partly recycled paper
and published and bound in Wales by
Y Lolfa Cyf., Talybont, Ceredigion SY24 5HE
e-mail ylolfa@ylolfa.com
website www.ylolfa.com
tel 01970 832 304
fax 832 782

Foreword

RICHARD LEWIS ENTERED THE world of television early in the 1960s, a formative time for broadcasting in Wales. There was no BBC Wales as such, and both radio and TV in the Welsh 'region' consisted of opt outs from the London based network services. It was a good time for people possessed of the pioneering spirit, or those who simply did not know what to do with themselves.

Lewis fell into the latter category. Having graduated, he had taken up teaching but knew he did not wish to make this his career. One day he applied for a fairly modest job with the BBC in Cardiff, and to his great surprise found himself being interviewed by the head of programmes, no less, and other top brass. Being hired by the BBC, in any position, was something of an achievement in those days.

Richard Lewis – invariably known as 'Dic' at the BBC, although he has always disliked the abbreviated form of his Christian name – made steady progress through the ranks. He had a spell as floor manager, the human link between the TV director in his 'gallery' and the performers facing the cameras. It proved invaluable experience, for at that time the BBC in Wales was providing several plays every year for the network from its Cardiff drama studio, a draughty converted chapel in the Roath area of the city. And these, mark you, were LIVE productions, with all the hazards that implies. Some years would elapse before every such programme would be recorded on tape and, after careful editing and refining, stored safely away before being released to the world.

Even more surprising for Lewis was his introduction to the frantic world of newsgathering. He had never seen himself as a journalist, and wondered how he would adapt when attached to a daily news programme. He learned how to keep cool in a crisis, and much else besides. His account of his days meeting deadlines, and recollections of the personalities involved in compiling and presenting the bulletins, provide an intriguing glimpse into the way things were learned 'on the hoof'.

The dawn of the 1970s saw the Welsh arm of the BBC – by then officially entitled BBC Wales – installed in its spacious HQ on the fringe of Cardiff, with Richard Lewis one of a talented team of TV producer directors producing an array of documentaries and dramas which were broadcast not only in Wales but right across the UK network. His subjects included the 'Welsh fasting girl' of Victorian times (Sarah Jacob) and the extraordinary evangelist Evan Roberts, who inspired the tempestuous religious revival of 1904. There was also a memorable re-creation of the last days of Dylan Thomas in America, and a brave portrayal of John Jenkins – entitled *The Extremist* – who opposed the Investiture of Charles as Prince of Wales and believed that the cause of Welsh independence justified acts of violence against property.

TV directors are by nature restless people who, just as they cut snappily from shot to shot in their productions, tend to move swiftly from one project to another. They rarely sit down to tell us how they actually go about their work. This book is unusual in that it is an insider's account of the business, written in a plain style and with attention to detail. The author tells us how he set about making particular programmes, the challenges they presented and the complexities of shooting schedules. Television may have moved on lately (or gone back, some might say), but the rationale of programme making remains unchanged. It sometimes involves doing the nearly impossible, but somehow the obstacles are surmounted and the programme goes out.

Richard Lewis, retired now, was a TV man of his time, but what he says is relevant to the practitioners of today. It's as well for them to know not just how things were done in the far from distant past, but the assumptions behind the output. The people who launched BBC Wales believed they could best serve the network by providing it with programmes about Wales and her people, and the big shots in Television Centre went along with this. In the era of Dr Who and Torchwood, which do immense credit to Welsh production standards but could be shot anywhere, the thinking appears to have changed – more in London, perhaps, than in Cardiff.

Herbert Williams

Preface

I HAVE ALWAYS FELT THAT to write an autobiography must be the ultimate form of conceit, best left to those for whom self-publicity is the primary driving force in their existence. You know the type – all 'piss and wind' as they say in Rhondda, all promotion and very little substance. Some of these have travelled far and achieved great honours based on very little other than this drive for self-promotion and recognition by others. In my case, I was taught to listen, to consider, to assess and definitely not say anything – unless it was *worth* saying. This nonconformist, somewhat puritanical approach coloured my early life and led me later to cloak any reminiscence in the indirect form of poetry so as not to offend! It also, doubtless, had the effect of limiting any early confidence I might have possessed, whilst others, less inhibited, charged ahead… but more of this later! Only now, having passed my 'seventieth year to Heaven' as Dylan might have said, have I succumbed to family exhortations to 'Write it down before it's too late!' Well here goes! I shall try not to bore you. Honest!

Richard Lewis

CHAPTER 1

Between Valley Walls and the War

MINE WAS A CAESAREAN birth, which is still evident in a small scalpel scar on my shoulder. The resultant traumatic, somewhat precipitate entrance to this world still reverberates in my being. My mother used to relate the story of the well-named Doctor Armstrong throwing her over his shoulder and carrying her to his car for the short journey to Pentwyn Cottage Hospital, because there were few ambulances available on 30 January 1938 and there was no time to lose! The revered Scottish medic was fond of the odd dram – hence the resultant scar...

I little knew that I was being born into a privileged household in what was then an idyllic community, in a valley on the verge of a catastrophic war. My parents both came from Cardiganshire: my mother, Lily May, from farming stock in Devil's Bridge, and my father, Lewis Haydn, from a family of seafarers in Aberaeron. They had met and married in Mynach chapel, Devil's Bridge, where my father had his first 'calling' to be a preacher, but had moved to Ton Pentre with its vast Jerusalem Methodist chapel. This huge temple to Methodism (now demolished) seated a congregation of a thousand and dominated the main street. For any aspiring preacher it was a prize worth gaining, particularly since it also boasted a newly built manse called 'Eryl' which had pride of place in one of the more select areas of Ton. Like the chapel, it boasted panelling of pitch pine and a grand staircase. It also had its own grounds, four bedrooms and electric lighting, at a time when gas or oil lighting was the norm. It was an ideal family home for my parents, who already had a daughter, Elsbeth Carol, born two years earlier. The house was sheltered in the lee of Maendy mountain, one of the last wooded areas of Rhondda Fawr. Many trees had been chopped down for pit props or fuel for industry, but Maendy, known to us children as 'God's little mountain', still maintained its farming and sprinkling of stunted trees which would provide an idyllic playground for us as children. We were surrounded by typical valley terraced houses, owned by colliers who responded to the daily hooter from Maendy Colliery – now sadly defunct and landscaped.

Lily and Haydn's marriage in Mynach Chapel, Devil's Bridge

Jerusalem's grim façade dominated the High Street…

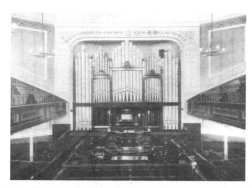

… contrasting with its rich interior and impressive organ

Proud mother and her two children

My father was joined by his formidable mother for this family portrait

Eryl, the chapel manse, and my home for eighteen years

LAMENT FOR A HOB-NAILED BOOT

No longer does
The hooter sound,
Its echoes from encircling hills
Rebound;
Nor colliers' hob-nailed boots
Their clatter sound
In sombre streets.
Nor do the chapels,
Large and grey,
Resound to hymns
Or sounds of men
Who pray.
No waggons roll
On inclines perilous and
Steep;
No tips appear
To threaten innocents
Asleep.
The Maendy's
Fern-clad slopes,
Her stunted trees
Our 'Sherwood' then,
Are carpeted with
Conifer and Spruce
To line the coffers
Of the money-men.
Though
Green and gold,
Her future seems assured,

As playground for the tourist
She'll be sold.
And yet,
To me,
Her heart no longer thrills
Or beats,
Since hob-nailed boots
Have ceased to clatter
Through her grey and tangled
Streets.

(RL *Poetry Now* 1990)

My early memories of life are strangely sunny (the calm before the storm, I suppose). The elegant house with its oil paintings (my father was a talented amateur artist as well as a musician) meant the ambience was scholarly. Books were very much in evidence; in fact they occupied every available square inch. My father spent most of his time reading or writing. He had graduated in theology from Aberystwyth University College and went from thence to Exeter College, Oxford to read for a Masters in Classics. I still have his reference books on Hebrew and Greek in my library. On the other hand, my mother, although a certificated teacher, dedicated her life to her children and her husband. For her, there was a kitchen to be scrubbed, a path or step to be washed, a family history to be told. Having suffered the considerable trauma of my birth, she never became pregnant again and we remained a two-child family. It was a sign of the times, since she had been one of ten and my father one of five.

Our house, Eryl, although large and detached, was built before the days of central heating and had fireplaces in every conceivable room – including the bedrooms. Normally we relied on a constant coal fire in the living room, an occasional one in the study and in bedrooms when we were ill. The outside coalhouse was very large and needed to be to cope with our winter coal consumption. This, doubtless, made us all fairly hardy, although we had frequent bouts of bronchitis, aggravated by the moist valley climate and my father's chain-smoking of the ubiquitous Woodbines. Indeed, chest hospitals were very much in vogue in the valleys as a result of the constant burning of 'King Coal'! Having said that, as children, we had instant access to the clean air and high hills where we spent most of our leisure time climbing trees, playing Cowboys and Indians and bathing in colliery feeder ponds.

Perhaps the most peculiar aspect of my early existence was speaking Welsh in what was then a largely English-speaking community. Both my parents were dedicated to the survival of the language, so at home we communicated in Cardiganshire Welsh. I only became aware of English when I went to Infants school and started making friends locally. I little knew then that my father was a prime mover in Welsh education in Rhondda and that, together with others, like the dynamic Kitchener Davies, had helped establish the first Welsh primary in Treorchy. In general, the local community consisted of people drawn from other mining areas such as England's North and South West who had been attracted by the vast expansion in the Welsh coalfield. Others had come from mid Wales or the North Wales quarries, helping to establish and sustain the Welsh nonconformist chapels, which, at that time, were like bookends on every street corner. This meant that spoken Welsh was rarely heard in our streets other than during and after chapel services. Even deacons seemed reluctant to use the language outside the walls of chapel and vestry. The 'Welsh Not' had been very successful in Rhondda and this, coupled with the huge influx of non-Welsh workers, almost stifled the language in the valley.

My earliest friends were, without exception, monoglot English – even those with very Welsh names. At the rear of every house in the valley there was an untreated lane or 'Gooly' (or was it 'Gwlie'!) which served as depository for bins and associated rubbish. It was in one of these that I discovered John, who was to become my best friend during my formative years. His parents ran a successful drapery business in Pentre. His father, although from the Tregaron area, spoke little Welsh but was still a stalwart of the congregational chapel. As an only child, John was heavily indulged by his parents and I don't think that mine were very keen on the friendship. The fact is that although my parents were living in a large rent-free house, their actual income was very small and they had none available to spend on 'indulgences'. I always remember that their grocery and butcher bills were always 'on the bill' which was always a struggle to reduce, or pay off, at the end of the month. On the other hand, I do not recall my father being without his Woodbines or being unable to buy a book he wanted. I concluded that my mother took the responsibility for balancing the books – in his favour of course... Having said that, I don't recall going without anything and in those austere, un-fashion-conscious days, clothes had to last a very long time.

The summer of '38 became an Indian summer as the nation prepared for war. By 1939 the number of gas lamps in our street and in the rest of the valley became noticeably fewer in number. Rhondda was 'battening down the hatches' for what was to be a very long war. Deacons became air-raid wardens or special constables; the ministry was under strain as able-bodied members were called up to the forces. The outlook for my father looked grim. What would the future hold for his children? Would there be a future? The prospect of a Britain under the Nazi jackboot seemed very real.

Blissfully unaware of most of this, I learned to walk in the empty streets, which are now lined with cars from Blaencwm to Porth. Very few were given petrol coupons which would sustain a car. In fact, I only remember there being one which belonged to a peripatetic schoolteacher in our street. In any event, my father never drove but relied on buses or trains and, later, a welcome lift in someone's car to conduct his ministry. We walked everywhere. The journey to my infants' school in Gelli, on which I was accompanied by my mother, was a good mile. It was on this journey that I first saw a Rhondda red double-decker bus and had my first traumatic experience of witnessing a dog being squashed on the road as it crossed in front of this leviathan. I have few memories of my time in the infants' school other than accidentally relieving my bladder on the girl at the next desk and the dank smell of the shelter beneath the school where we huddled whenever there was an air-raid warning. Nevertheless, I obviously learnt English without any problem and suddenly became bilingual, which is relatively easy at a young age when the brain mops up everything like a sponge.

I was certainly aware in the early 1940s of increasing war activity: aircraft overhead, searchlights and enforced blackouts at night. In fact, my sister and I spent many nights sleeping under the oak kitchen table, since this, coupled with a large corrugated iron sheet propped against the kitchen window, afforded our home's only protection. Some nights we stood in wonderment at the bedroom window watching the searchlights and flashes from explosions further down the cwm. We found out later that buildings like Ystrad Library had been demolished. Further raids devastated the nearby village of Cwmparc and many were killed. During the day, things were comparatively quiet, but I can still recall what must have been a lone Dornier bomber trailing smoke at a level much lower than the mountaintops, being pursued by an RAF fighter. After these events, we often scoured the mountains behind our house in the vain hope of finding some interesting scrap of wreckage! I certainly have vivid memories of local constabulary and Home Guardsmen rifle shooting with ancient Lee Enfields on Maendy mountain, whilst we children watched from a safe distance. As schoolchildren we also watched (again from a safe distance) as Field Marshal Montgomery ('Monty') came to nearby Maendy Barracks to inspect the troops.

In general, these were seen by us as halcyon times, since we did not understand the pressures suffered by our parents. We were happy to play, unencumbered by thoughts of the rights or wrongs of war. Our happiness was based on very little; we had toy guns and tricycles, but there were no sweet shops, chocolate was no longer on the shelves, and I don't think I saw a banana until 1946! School for me was not a happy experience. Ton junior school was unrelenting in its drive to teach the three R's – in English. Our teacher (whose name I intentionally cannot recall) was a martinet. If you couldn't recite a particular 'times table' of his choice, you were caned in front of the class. Arithmetic being my weakest subject meant I was caned often! It certainly gave me no love for that subject. Stubbornly, I never told my parents that I was subject to these regular beatings, and scars were presumably hidden or engrained on my brain. Any expertise I have now with money must be due to my Cardiganshire genes! My more formative education happened during weekends, when we played on the hills or in local streams...

RHONDDA TROUT

In dim and distant
'Forty-four',
When Axis legions thundered
On some foreign shore,
I fought my battles
Nearer home.

In stone and slurried
Landscape,
Down a lane
Beside a muddy trickle,
Brown and plain there ran
The Brook –
Along a dusty 'gwli' bare,
Where,

We as children
Launched our own beleaguered convoys
For a 'dare'.

As paper dreadnoughts
Fought the tide,
And missiles flew
From every side,
We played at
War.

In sodden socks
On slimy rocks
We'd fight it out,
Disturbing only
Placid
Coal-infested
Rhondda trout.

(RL Childhood memories 1944)

I cannot ignore the dominance of the chapel in all of this. Carol and I, as 'privileged' children of the manse, attended chapel dutifully three times every Sunday: morning service, Sunday School (Ysgol Sul) at two o'clock, then evening service at six. Scrubbed and dressed in 'Sunday best' we sat in a pew to the side of the Big Seat where the deacons sat. We were very exposed to the scrutiny of the rest of the large congregations of those times. We were not particularly stressed by this; for us, it was normality. We listened intently to whoever was preaching; playing the part without questioning what was being said. In those days, of course, four-part harmony was in its heyday and I enjoyed this aspect of the services. Jerusalem had a grand organ with a lovely mellow tone and its pipes, dominating the pulpit, impressed me greatly, to the extent that I would be drawn to try to master its secrets in my teens.

The deacons, old and severe, contrasted with my father who was comparatively young. They varied between those who supported my father's ideas and those who opposed him. 'Evans the Undertaker', a sweet and gentle soul, was very supportive and acted almost like the family odd-job man throughout my father's life in the ministry – and later, in times of professional need. On the other hand, 'Evans the Solicitor', a tall, grim, unsmiling lawyer, was a constant thorn in my father's side. These tensions did not pass un-noticed by myself or my sister.

After evening service, the younger members of the chapel would walk to Maendy Road, in the shadow of Maendy mountain, where later, in our teens, we would begin to experience the odd 'liaison'. Of course, chapel was not limited to the Sunday and there were other weekly meetings which had to be attended: *Cwrdd Gweddi* on a Monday, *Ysgol Gân* (choir practice), the young people's 'Band of Hope' and *Seiat* (prayer meeting) on a Thursday. We attended some but not all of these. Although I remember sitting a lone exam in the chapel library, somehow I absorbed very little religious knowledge, doubtless a reaction against having too much of it. I am still pretty slow to answer crossword clues relating to religion or its history…

COMMUNION (Jerusalem Chapel)

How strange it was
To me,
A child
Grey-suited to the knee,
Strait-jacketed by
Brown,
Embracing,
Varnished pews of
Nonconformity;
When, suddenly,
A shroud would lift
To show myriad
Dancing silver cups,
Those earthly symbols of
The Holy Trinity.

To see such magic
In this sombre place,
The red,
The silver and
The Gold,
Was proof enough
To one not yet inspired
Or yet old,
That God was here;
Not just His spirit, but
His face.

(RL Personal Poems)

I was never convinced that my father actually had 'responded to the call', although he never admitted any reservations to us and preached to congregations with great fervour and authority and was much in demand. I think his problem was that he was the youngest son of a domineering Welsh mam from Aberaeron, who was a convert of the Evan Roberts 1904 Revival in New Quay. Wife of a sea captain and early widow of the same (he died from some foreign bug at sea off the west coast of Africa and his body was brought home for burial in Aberarth), my paternal grandmother was the Welsh matriarch personified. Determined not to lose her bright youngest to either the sea or wars (the First World War was raging), she ensured that he would avoid the call-up by studying for the church. This was not unusual in those times. His older brothers, however, made their careers mainly at sea, except in the case of Arnold, who became a merchant banker in the City. These 'captain's genes' may account for my later desire to be the boss (though I don't think I inherited Arnold's financial abilities). My father was also, in a way, captain of his particular ship – Jerusalem – with a motley and often rebellious crew! Although he was faithful to his congregation, his responsibilities, and, apparently, to his God, I am still not totally convinced that he wouldn't have been happier in his books as an Oxford don. In that case, he would never have met my mother and yours truly would not have been born. Isn't fate strange!

The big break from all this over indulgence in things religious came every summer when we escaped to the country. It was not much of a break for my father; he had arranged to preach in various Cardiganshire chapels every Sunday since we needed the money. We always went to Aberaeron (then anglicised as 'Aberayron') or Devil's Bridge; the former being my father's sister's home and the latter my maternal parents' farm. This journey was an annual pilgrimage and the preparations began several days before. The large cardboard trunk was packed with every conceivable or necessary article of clothing for the four of us. Sundry other cases were also filled. One day before the journey, the trunk was transported (by courtesy of some willing chapel member with a vehicle) to Ystrad railway station. The following day, the epic journey began:

1. Train to Blaenrhondda – change to
2. Train through the tunnel to Port Talbot
   – connection to
3. Train to Carmarthen – change to
4. Train to Aberystwyth via Strata Florida station.

Some eight hours later we would arrive exhausted at the bleak and strangely silent Strata station where my similarly quiet, pipe-smoking grandfather would meet us with his pony and trap. Another 45 minutes through country lanes and stunning scenery would bring us to Penlonfedw, the family farm. I will always remember the warmth of its open fire and the tranquillity, broken only by the sound of free-range chickens and the occasional cry of the curlew or skylark. This would be our Welsh-speaking paradise for the next month, broken only by a short visit (via two buses) to Aberaeron to see the other *mam-gu* and her (also rather severe) daughter, Elaine.

We normally spent most of the summer in Devil's Bridge (we seemed to have long summers those days), where the welcome was warm and the children's days seemed longer and more idyllic. I would spend most of the day with the cows, ponies and pigs, or playing with my cousin David in his parents' house, Rhiwmynach, in the village, often not going back to the farm till dark. My God, was it dark! There were no streetlights, unlike Rhondda, and unless there happened to be a moon, one had to literally feel the way home. But in those days, the countryside was safe and the sounds of war were not evident in North Cardiganshire. Lighting in the home depended on candles, oil-lamps or the later pressurised Tilley Lamps. I can still smell that pungent oil. There was of course no television, very few radios (which had to have their wet-batteries charged in Aberystwyth) and no alarm clocks – just the sound of the cock's crow to wake you in the morning. Travel was by means of pony, pony and trap or *gambo* (cart), with the very occasional commercial van which serviced the farm shop being the only mechanical device seen.

The farm was a safe paradise for us children, overseen by our diminutive but hardy grandmother, Sarah Ann. I never heard her speak English, though her ancestors came to Plynlimon from Dumfries in Scotland in 1650. Lewis MacMazon was a drover who migrated (with his sheep) to settle in the hills at Llerneuaddau, near Ponterwyd. One of his descendants was Sir John Rhys, Oxford scholar and leading Welsh academic. MacMazon later became Mason; although his subsequent children adopted the Christian name Lewis as their surname. One of his offspring, Richard (born 1850), married Jane Morgan from Cwmergyr, and my grandmother came from that union. Their home was Erwbarfe, a large sheep farm in the mountains. But Sarah Ann was to marry David from Penlonfedw, who had opened a general provisions shop on his smallholding. He was a quiet but highly respected member of nearby Mynach Methodist chapel which, incidentally and fortuitously, was to be my father's first calling as minister after his student days. It was here that he met my mother Lily May, one of ten children raised at Penlonfedw. It was a brisk courtship and they were married at Mynach chapel.

So it was a busy Penlonfedw that I remember. There were animals to feed, fields to mow and hay to be stacked – all social events when everybody lent a hand. The shop demanded daily attention from the women because my grandfather also had a daily 'round' of nearby farms and villages, delivering goods to the locals. During the war years, this was done with the assistance of an old Austin car which had a large box affixed to the rear. I still remember the stench of grandfather's pipe in the car, added to the exhaust fumes which seemed to emanate from the gearbox. The welcome he received from the Welsh-speaking farmers was warm and the conversations illuminating. I would spend many hours in this car, relieved by mugs of tea or homemade cake. He spoke very little to me, but the warmth of his personality is still etched in my memory. My sister Carol would spend her day with cousin Mary (Mali) from Rhiwmynach, who as Mary Lloyd Jones would become one of Wales' leading painters. We all met at the end of the day and enjoyed a farmhouse supper in Penlonfedw. In those pre-supermarket days, food was all locally produced; large salted hams hung in the shop, butter and cheese were prepared in the dairy, and rabbits shot with a 12-bore in the fields. The air in the farm smelt fresh, rich and good. It was with some reluctance that we would board the battered, green Crosville bus for the inevitable transfer via Aberystwyth to my aunt's house in Aberaeron.

Although I liked the harbour town with its beaches and riverside, I was aware, even as a child, that relationships were (shall we say) a little strained. My aunt Elaine was a tall, somewhat severe spinster of that parish, a pillar of the local community, chapel organist, head of domestic science in Aberaeron and a staunch supporter of the Liberal Party. For her, children were an embarrassment, best confined to school, definitely seen but not heard. Because of this, we were often farmed out to relatives or neighbours at bedtime, although all our meals were eaten in Newholme. She was, by nature and profession, a superb cook, which ensured that our table sagged under the weight of delicious tarts, cakes and trifles even during the war years.

Much as I enjoyed all this, I welcomed the daily escape to river or beach to mix with friends I had made locally. One of these was Gareth Owen, son of the headmaster, who would later become a solicitor and much-respected local historian. He was a fine tennis player and athlete who died in his prime from a particularly virulent cancer – a sad loss to the community. I returned to the Tabernacle chapel to attend his funeral.

Because my father was raised in Aberaeron he was an excellent swimmer, fly-fisherman and shooter, of shotguns in particular. Many an evening was spent on the River Aeron where I watched him fish for the local trout, sewin and salmon. We often strayed into private land in Llanerchaeron (now run by the National Trust) when the local squire Ponsonby-Lewis, much to my father's chagrin, would chase us away with his shotgun.

Proud owner of a trendy
corduroy jacket

Proud poacher with two fish
caught in Llanerchaeron

On holiday in Aberaeron…

… and on the beach in Borth

My father considered that he, as a local boy, had divine right of access to these waters, to an extent that he never bought a fishing licence.

After these weeks of idyllic peace we had to face the laborious return train journey to the valley and its proximity to war. Barrage balloons still floated, anchored above some of the run-down parks, and military vehicles could be seen clattering through the narrow streets. But still, life went on. I remember fundraising garden parties given by a local doctor and family picnics in the hills with neighbours. There were still choral evenings though choirs were more mixed than previously, many tenors and baritones being at war in Europe. There were still rousing 'big meetings' (*cwrdde mawr*) with guest preachers raising the chapel rafters with colourful oratory, which is where I must have had my first taste of DRAMA! On such days not even the pews could accommodate the congregation; extra benches had to be brought in from the adjacent vestry. They were memorable times, never to be repeated...

As the war dragged on, I became more aware of relatives who were in action: Uncle Lel (Llewelyn) from Cilie Aeron suffered the battle at El Alamein and was thereafter very subdued by shell shock; uncles Jink (Jenkin) and Hywel were captains in the Navy. These were some of my heroes as the war, and my time at primary school, came to an end.

I well remember the closing years of the war, particularly when there was a huge influx of American forces who were billeted in the valley pending their involvement in the coming invasion of Nazi Europe. None were put up at Eryl since my father was opposed to any war. Had he not been a minister he would have been a conscientious objector. Nevertheless, I met some Yanks. Two were lodged with my friend John and his parents. Bristling with armaments, they were very kind and generous with their gum and chocolate Hershey Bars. I was thrilled by the guns in particular. This also was probably when I first saw a black man, from the American South, billeted in another house nearby. There had been no black people in Rhondda before then, although the colliers' coal-black faces coming off shift might have suggested otherwise.

As the invasion date approached, the actual sounds of war seemed less evident and my parents scoured the daily *Western Mail* for news of progress in Europe. The radio was still the main source of news. We got letters from uncles abroad – including a regular copy of the *National Geographic*. (This gave me an enduring interest in geography which has proved useful in solving my wife's crosswords!)

1945 saw the climax of things military. I heard the announcement of Peace in Europe (VE Day) on my father's radio in Eryl. Was it spoken by John Snagge or Alvar Liddell? I can't remember! Later I was to hear a similar announcement in August on my Uncle Sammy's wet accumulator battery radio in Devil's Bridge when VJ Day was announced. There were enormous celebrations in the Rhondda when peace was declared. As children, we were heavily involved in the parties which occurred up and down every street in the borough. Trestle tables were set up and bedecked with flowers, jellies and lemonade. I think I was sick. The relief was tangible.

Little did we realise then that the post-war years

would be harsh, grey and austere. Many men had died in the war, businesses had suffered, congregations had been decimated and there was little food available. The ration book and its coupons were king. But then, I was growing up and facing my next real challenge: the scholarship exam!

CHAPTER 2

Gwell Dysg na Golud
Better Scholarship than Riches

THE LAST YEARS OF the 1940s passed uneventfully, apart from some events that stick in the memory. Winter 1947 produced a snowfall that has scarcely been matched, before or since. The snow lay some six feet deep in the valley and remained for several weeks. The council cut trenches through the streets so that people could walk to work or the shops; these white cliffs became almost a permanent feature. The house froze and so did we. Schools were closed and as a growing lad (growing out of trousers quicker than my mother could extend them), I discovered the delights of being ill, or slightly ill, in bed: reading *Just William*, Enid Blyton mysteries, comics and encyclopaedias. My mother was neurotic about health and had read extensively about this or that symptom. Consequently, she was a pushover when I started performing the part of a dying swan; I would be sent to bed with a coal fire and hot water bottle. My father was more sceptical, although he often took to his bed with some obscure 'colitis' and was dosed with 'slippery elm' – an apparent panacea!

FRAMED CALVARY
(A childhood memory of three telegraph posts seen on
Gelli Mountain in 1949)

When, as a youth,
Then sickly, thin and pale,
Much given to
Malingering
Abed with
Rover, *Dandy*, or
Some simple tale
Of heroes
Bold and
True,
To pass the time
Or help to ease a
Cold or
'Flu;
I scarcely ever paused
For thoughts on
Growing old.
But, even then,
My thoughts would venture
To infinity.

Beyond the curtained bay,
The valley walls
Loomed large and grey,
Where, on a ridge,
There stood a
Ghostly Trinity;

Three posts,
Three crossbars,
Which, to me,
Will always be
My very own,
My very private
Calvary.

(RL: Rhondda in retrospect)

I became an avid reader, sustained with regular refuelling by my mother and her snacks. She knew the importance of books; she had been a qualified teacher, though her taste had become limited to the *Woman's Weekly* which she had delivered. I received the *Dandy* and *Beano* comics, whilst father stuck to *Y Goleuad* or *Y Cymro*.

When recovered, I reluctantly returned to Ton primary to be beaten into submission once more by a teacher who was either getting gratification from it or was determined to get me through the inevitable scholarship exam. It was a boys' school, partitioned from the girls'. At around this time, I became infatuated from afar with an older boy who seemed to me to epitomise beauty – a virtual Adonis. I never spoke to him or approached him, merely loved his image from afar. His very presence would arise feelings in my groin that were very confusing. I suppose it all meant that my hormones were 'on the move' and I was never to have this feeling for a male subsequently. Of course, I never shared any of this with my parents, who presumably thought someone else would educate me about sex. Sex was not on the home curriculum, in spite of the fact that my sister Carol had got into Porth County Girls' and was aware of sexual differences. I didn't feel challenged by her success in passing the scholarship exam with flying colours. There was no sibling rivalry and we were good friends to the end.

I spent a lot of my time daydreaming and fantasising, fuelled by escapist games on the mountains with John. We became very taken by radio – particularly the Light Programme which aired such gems as *ITMA* (*It's That Man Again*), *Variety Bandbox*, *Dick Barton – Special Agent* and later *The Goon Show*. These quickly overtook *Children's Hour*, which we should presumably have been following. There was also the occasional Welsh Home Service programme like *SOS Galw Gari Tryfan* or *Noson Lawen*, to which my father responded to with gales of laughter – rare for him. Since John's parents were relatively well off, he would eventually get a new reel-to-reel recorder on which we devised our own Goon Shows, with us imitating the characters and inventing suitable sound effects. This was the beginning of what would be, for us both, a career in broadcasting. But I digress...

In 1949 came the dreaded scholarship exam, with my mother trying her best to coach me in both English and maths. I don't remember my father in this context. He presumably sat in his study and worried. There was plenty for him to worry about at that time. Came the day. Would I survive the ordeal?

I had recently developed a tendency to have acute hay fever in summer months, and several of my maternal grandmother's family suffered from asthma. Would I be able to concentrate for the three hours of tension this exam demanded? Miraculously, I passed

– including the dreaded maths! The top ninety in the Rhondda, according to the system in those days, would go to Porth County Grammar School for Boys, one of the best in Wales; the rest would be consigned to what was considered by many a horror of a secondary school. I came 29th in the Rhondda; my friend John was top!

This system did not always mean you had to stay in the school to which you were assigned; you could, with effort, be transferred up to the grammar school. My mother's doctor, Tony Lloyd, initially went to Pentre Secondary, but gained a place in higher education through subsequent effort. Dewi Griffiths, ace BBC Sports director, also emerged from Pentre Secondary, going on to big responsibilities with the Beeb.

So there I was. Somehow I had made it. I would join my sister (who attended the adjoining girls' school) the following autumn, though I scarcely saw her, only occasionally 'on the buses' as you might say. I couldn't wait to don the grey flannels, the cap and blazer (with its badge and motto: *Gwell Dysg na Golud*) and wait for the morning school bus and the half-hour journey to Porth. I had absolutely no reservations. This was to be the 'Big Adventure'. My parents were delighted, my father... surprised. I believe I was to get my first bicycle, a red and slightly heavy upright model, which was more than they could afford. My friend John had a black, drop-handlebar, sporting model. But there was no rivalry, and we spent the summer days racing around the valley. I haven't been as energetic since then. After the summer holidays (again partially spent in Cardiganshire) I joined the throng awaiting the bus on the first day of term.

Informal pose on the first day of school

Formal studio photograph, common in the days before instamatic cameras

The journey was memorable. Excited newcomers mixed with the old stagers as the red double-decker lurched through Ystrad, Llwynypia and Tonypandy before arriving in Cemetery Road where both schools were sited.

The girls were dropped off before the boys, who

then had to climb a steep access road to the school. We assembled on a tarmac area, known as 'the field', to the rear of school and waited in trembling lines. We were then separated into forms A, B, C and D according to results. I was in A. Once established in our classroom we were given our first shock. We would be given a timetable of subjects, requiring us to scurry around from classroom to classroom (or laboratory) and from teacher to teacher. Now this was new! We waited, with bated breath, to see what kind of teachers we would get. Would they have a cane? Would I be beaten? Of course, within the first week we were to see all the teachers who taught the lower school. They were a motley crowd, mostly dressed in flowing black graduate gowns, some with canes at the ready. The headmaster, William Howells (MSc), was a tiny figure who seemed to be wearing a dark toupee – although, in reality, I think it was just his haircut. His deputy, TR Davies, was tall, thin and grim, with a cane much in evidence. He was the active disciplinarian in the school, who spent most of his day patrolling the corridors, whipping his cane from side to side, chastising or tweaking the ears of passing pupils. Senior mathematics master was Benson. He had a glass eye but no cane; he only needed his one eye to silence any pupil of any age. Isn't discipline a strange thing? We even feared him in the sixth form! Mr Thomas (known as 'Boxer') taught history. He only had one lung (having suffered a gas attack in the World War I trenches) and coughed constantly. He would enter the classroom, throw open every available window and exclaim (to nobody in particular), 'This place smells like a stale lavatory!'

Other teachers were younger or less colourful. It

must have been difficult staffing schools with so many men lost to the war. I remember Vernon Jones well (or 'Santos' as he was known by the boys because of his Spanish moustache), who was later to become the last headmaster of Porth before it became a comprehensive. He was fun and I still correspond with him. Mr Owen was the Welsh teacher; a sad, tall, white-haired North Walian who looked a little out of place but was a gentle soul. I was never taught by Mr Rochat since he taught Spanish. He had a formidable reputation as teacher and produced many star pupils who became university professors.

Mr Morris taught PE. He was a thin, slightly balding man, who wore a baggy brown sweater and a muffler in the winter, which was swapped for an old cricket sweater in the summer. This was in the days before trendy sportswear and he was never seen in shorts. I think he must have been a sergeant in the First World War. I was definitely not attracted to him. In fact, hating all contact sports or anything involving leaping or jumping (I would have been stuck in Colditz), I tried to chicken out of PE. If I couldn't work the old 'dying swan/terminal cough' trick then I ensured (easily) that there would be a sick note available from my gullible mother. Surprisingly, I became quite fond of tennis and cricket, being a passable batsman; but generally, my interest in sport was tied to my need to impress the girls after school or at weekends. I have noticed of late that my friends who showed an active interest in energetic sports like jogging or squash haven't made it to their early sixties. Some who I met later in reunions sported sticks or Zimmer frames; but this may all be coincidental. Morris 'Gym' did not last beyond our middle school years; he died of cancer, presumably brought on by his Capstan Full Strength habit. As pupils we all, surprisingly, walked in crocodile over the next hill to witness his interment in Porth Cemetery. This may have been a move by the headmaster to warn us all of the horrors of tobacco. In the event it was unsuccessful, since smoke continued to rise from the boys' toilets with an undiminished density. In those days practically all men smoked; it was a necessary badge of adulthood.

In true public school style, Porth County referred to everyone by abbreviating their names to initials or some diminutive form of their Christian name. I became known (much to my parents' annoyance) as Dick. This habit would continue in the BBC in later life (shades of the Civil Service) although I would sign myself in the Welsh style as DIC. My father was inconsolable and hated this very English fashion for abbreviation. So my world became populated by TR or CJ or some such letters…

As the timetable commenced, I quickly realised that there were subjects to love and those to be loathed. I enjoyed English, Latin and French; finding the latter very similar to Welsh with many words in common. The teachers were also nice. History was not interesting, since it almost exclusively dealt with English kings and queens, with no mention of Welsh leaders or their battles. Arithmetic continued to mystify me, being joined by the slightly less challenging geometry (I understood shapes), but I was totally floored by trigonometry and algebra, which made no sense at all! I was, however, captivated by the newness and technical glitter of the laboratories. The Bunsen burners, the retorts and glass pipework were a world away from the musty books in the manse.

I became determined to get involved, to get a white coat and join the 'boffins' of the new world. My father was not pleased. Apart from its base line philosophy of good classics teaching, there was a definite bias towards science in Porth – a post-war reaction to an increasingly technological society. The list of alumni in Porth includes many who have achieved great things, gained glittering prizes and become leaders of society. This was not surprising, since the school could cream off the best of any valley generation. Among the names are: Sir Ben Bowen Thomas (Chairman of UNESCO, Paris), Dr Alun Oldfield Davies (BBC controller), Mansel Thomas (composer), Gareth Griffiths (international rugby player), Gwyn Thomas (novelist, broadcaster and humorist), as well as literally legions of esteemed doctors, lawyers, leaders of commerce and captains of industry, scientists, even broadcasters! (See Owen Vernon Jones' book on Porth County.)

The language of the school was English. In the morning service English hymns were sung; you were even caned in English. The only moment when Welsh was recognised was on Saint David's Day, as I would discover to my cost (as one of the four or five Welsh speakers) when poems were recited or songs sung. Since I was passable boy soprano I was often chosen to perform, and on one ghastly occasion I forgot the lyrics – being inaudibly prompted by Mr Owen's stage whisper. I wasn't the star of that particular show. I assume that fellow Welshmen Cennard Davies (academic) Arfon Williams (master of the 'englyn') and David Enoch (psychiatrist) went through the same hell.

At that time, of course, I accepted that this was the way of the world; not thinking that this was a very biased, anglicised approach to education. You may have been wondering why I have written this book in English, but since two thirds of my professional career was in that language and most of my crews on network epics were monoglot English, I thought it made sense.

We spent our daily breaks up on the tarmac 'field', taunting the girls next door through the separating wire fence; or, more likely in later years, admiring their brown limbs as they played netball or rounders in their navy knickers. Our meals were eaten in regimental fashion in the school refectory. It was stodgy fare with the inevitable semolina pudding and the occasional (welcome) jam sponge and custard. These could be supplemented by snacks, including sweets and chocolates, from the tuck shop inside the gates, run by the caretaker and his wife. This is where my tooth rot began. I was to be taken regularly by my mother to Dr Guttman (or some-such spelling), a German dentist who later changed his name to Goodwin in order not to offend his patients who were still reeling from the effects of war. He was a great believer in extraction, with the aid of gas, and would whip out my teeth at the slightest provocation. I probably got brain damage thanks to his preoccupation with gas, which certainly didn't give me many 'laughs'. He was also a great believer in gold fillings which required him to gouge out most of a tooth first. I can still hear the drill. Most of these were later to fall out, leaving me with several yawning gaps in my smile. My mother, of course, was a devout follower of all things medical and never missed an appointment. More's the pity. It certainly taught me to be not only a patient – but *patient*. I find myself now able to suffer minor pains as well as most.

Music only received cursory attention in our timetable; I think we had an elderly lady (peripatetic) once a week. Art or painting was similarly at the lower end of the school's priorities; although I had inherited a little talent in both from my father and mother – who was no mean hand with a pencil and sketchbook. As I mentioned, although I had some ability as a boy soprano this was not nurtured in school and only emerged in chapel services. I did commence piano lessons at this time, walking to a Welsh-speaking Cardiganshire-born piano teacher who would spend most of the lesson describing his country childhood. I was certainly not under pressure from him and subsequently advanced very slowly through the grades. Nevertheless, I was intrinsically interested in music and we often listened to the many classical records we had in Eryl – the *New World Symphony* being a particular favourite. Inevitably, I would, as minister's son, be expected to compete in local eisteddfodau, but I don't recall receiving any laurels for this. Usually, children who were coached by their parents shone in these circumstances, but I was expected to make my own way.

In any event, as I advanced into adolescence, my voice quickly dropped to almost bass-baritone. This would be very handy for the spoken word, but somewhat limited me as to a repertoire of songs. Of course, I had no ideas for my future when attending the early years in Porth, except to join the 'white-coat brigade' in the laboratories as, possibly, a nuclear scientist. Even as children we were becoming aware of the nuclear threat with the commencement of the Cold War. I well remember a vivid poster I designed for a class debate being banned by my form teacher. It was full of ghastly reds and purple blotches representing nuclear clouds. I also remember getting into more hot water in class by sketching cartoons (in the teacher's absence) of various staff members on the blackboard. I was quite good at this and had a ready audience, until discovered by the said form teacher and suffering the inevitable 'gym dap' on the bottom! This didn't actually stop my delight in cartooning or lampooning colleagues which lasted well into my professional career at the BBC.

Gareth Price, Buddha-like, as Head of Programmes

Geraint Stanley Jones – I can't remember the occasion, but the film title might provide a clue

S4C was taking over as the dominant commissioning body

(*I don't know where HTV got the idea that we are undermining their position...*)

I won't bore you with detail, but I easily continued into form 2A, rather through native cunning than hard work. The timetable continued much as before, though my life was upset by one particular event – the sudden death of my friend John's father. This meant that John spent many days having meals with us whilst his mother tried to cope with funeral arrangements and the prospect of having to run the drapery businesses in Pentre and Treorchy. It was a seminal moment in John's life and thenceforth he became somewhat of a 'latch-key' child and was frequently missing from the classroom. Luckily, he was *very* bright and his future career did not suffer from interruptions in his formal education.

1951 saw the much-trumpeted Festival of Britain held largely in London on the South Bank of the Thames and in Battersea; although there were other more local celebrations. My father was curious and determined that we should see these events first hand. We therefore all travelled by GWR steam express then via the underground to spend a week in the then Celtic Hotel, Russell Square (run by a deacon in Jewin Welsh

Chapel) and days with various relatives. I saw my first red neon sign – flashing above the hotel entrance. This, coupled with the mammoth display in Piccadilly Circus made a deep impression on me.

The Festival centred around the 'Dome of Discovery' which was crammed with futuristic exhibits and surrounded by other pavilions concentrating on other aspects of 'Modern Britain'. I was, as an adolescent, equally impressed by a centrepiece 'erection' called the 'Skylon', made from steel and wire and pointing skywards. Since my own hormones were again on the move and I was experiencing 'bodily development', I found it highly significant. The only structure that now remains is the Royal Festival Hall which we visited then to see a performance of *Swan Lake*. In all, I found the week hard going, only relaxing in Battersea Funfair. I had been too busy, consuming strange food from hot self-service restaurants (where you lifted a flap to select your chosen dishes) and over-consumption of pop. We dutifully went to Ealing (by tube) to see Uncle Arnold and his wife Peggy; then to the end of the line – Cockfosters – to visit Aunty Eirlys and husband Eric, with their son Warwick at Enfield. I was glad to get back to join the comparative normality of school where I could relax.

It was around this time that my friends and I began to attend Saturday cinema in either the Workmen's Hall, Ton, or the Grand, a fleapit in nearby Pentre. John and I were both instant fans of the moving picture and lapped up all the cartoons and Hal Roach comedies shown at that time. Chaplin became our hero, and we imitated his walk ad nauseam. John even befriended the somewhat sad projectionist at the Grand, a Sellers-like character (as seen in *The Smallest Show on Earth*) who occasionally let us watch in the projection room as he struck the massive carbon arc to flood the huge screen with magic. We were captivated and totally absorbed by this new medium. You must remember that these were days when radio was still king. Television was rarely seen in people's homes until Coronation Day, after which it became popular with those who could afford a set. We couldn't. In fact, we only ever had a wire-fed black and white rental set which only showed two flickering channels.

As with all new toys, John was determined to have the latest and soon persuaded his mother to get him a projector, albeit a rather simple version – a 9.5 Pathescope hand-cranked model with low voltage light. Still, we spent hours cranking this to produce its faint monochrome (sepia) images, with all our other friends being jealous. Such was John's influence on his mother that he would soon persuade her to cut holes between their two attics to create a projection room and cinema. Later, as he up-graded the equipment, first to 8mm then to silent 16mm, we began to invite gullible friends to 'film shows' at his house. We even charged them pennies for show. John would be projectionist and I would be usherette with torch, but fortunately minus the frilly costume! What fun we had, even creating posters and serving drinks to our sceptical customers. We became avid cinemagoers since this was our first real opportunity to escape the valley and enter the ever-widening land of our imagination. We soon discovered that, with dedication and a few shillings, it was possible to see six different programmes in various nearby cinemas in any given week. There were the two in Ton and Pentre, one in Gelli, and others in Tonypandy and Treorchy; all with plush red seats and a ticket to childhood heaven!

Strangely, although John was the enabler of all this, he would forge a career largely in radio whereas I would end up in television. It took a few years for me to get even a stills camera (via mail order on the 'never-never') but I soon caught up, buying a Kodak 8mm (hand-wound) cine camera, then a Bell and Howell 3-lens turret model and, finally, a sophisticated 16mm zoom model. I made several films during my teens including one on the Urdd camp in Llangrannog lasting some 45 minutes. Among the films we saw in the early '50s were Laurence Olivier's *Henry V* and *A Matter of Life and Death*. I found the latter quite scary, but then it was full of medical sequences which reminded me of the dentist! On Saturdays when we weren't at the cinema, we would often perform plays on a raised area in John's back garden; again, often to a reluctant audience of friends. Nevertheless, we imagined the plots and staged the action and I suppose it was all formative in our development. I would sometimes perform in my father's mini dramas in Jerusalem's large vestry to a capacity audience. I had a love-hate relationship with drama: I loved to be on, but hated getting on the stage. But then, stage fright is fairly common, even amongst the top professionals today.

Meanwhile, back at the 'Ranch', as the prefabricated lower school was known, my formal education continued into forms 3A and 4A. During this time I remember attending a speech day with the whole school in a large chapel in Porth. There, illustrious members of the school were awarded cups for effort in academic subjects or in sport. I can tell you that I was not one of these, merely an appreciative member of the audience. However, I was suitably impressed by a sixth-former, John Cynan Jones, who played the organ and was later to become conductor of the world-renowned Treorchy Male Voice Choir. This made me become even more determined to try my hand at playing the organ. Being of a devious nature, I crept into Jerusalem one Saturday morning (its doors were always open in those vandal-free days) and headed for the organ bench. All was silent, apart from the ticking of the large clock and some clunking from the radiators warming the chapel in readiness for the Sunday services. I threw on the appropriate switches which I had observed from my pole position in the family pew, and struck a chord. Empowered by the response, I pulled out various stops, tentatively feeling for the pedals with my feet. Wow! I was thrilled by the almost physical effect of the vibration and echo. I continued in this vein for almost ten minutes before I eventually reversed the switches and crept out...

I was naïve to think that no-one else would hear this unscheduled recital. The chapel caretaker, whose house adjoined the chapel, had been a silent witness to my organic debut. He was to report me to the deacons on the morrow. My father, who had to 'face the music' that Sunday, was surprised but, I think, not totally displeased. He later arranged for one of the organists, Mrs Reynolds, to give me a lesson once a week. She was a good teacher and taught me to 'feel' for the pedal notes as I mastered the simple, then more complicated hymn tunes. Since then, I never really looked down much at the pedals when playing, although I notice many so-called 'professional organists' have heads bobbing up and down like proverbial yo-yos. This interest in the organ lasted throughout my life and I played in various chapels ranging from Carmarthen (Heol Dŵr) to Tŷ Ddewi (Tabernacle) and Cardiff's Crwys Methodist Chapel. We still have a two-manual organ in our flat. God help the neighbours! I have, much to the amusement of film crews, tried grand organs when on location, such as those in Swansea's Brangwyn Hall or Saint David's Cathedral. It's very showbiz to 'make 'em laugh, make 'em cry' but I never could resist the challenge! Jerusalem has now been demolished and nothing remains...

Built by *Vowles of Bristol*, the organ was opened in 1918, had 28 stops and a beatiful mellow tone.

VOX HUMANA

The serried ranks
Are silent
Now;
The piccolo,
The Bourdon and
The Flute —
Mute
Witnesses of
Crumbling pulpit and of
Pew.

No wind blows
Through,
Since bellows breathed
Their last
For congregations and
For voices long since
Passed.
The transient
Holy Wind which swept
This vale
Now moans through
Fractured casements,
All
For sale.

(RL Rhondda in retrospect)

During my period in 4A and the lead up to 'O' levels, I shot up in height and soon became one of the tallest in the form. Conscious of this, I became a follower of the Charles Atlas school (the muscle-bound man whose adverts showed him as having changed from one who had sand kicked in his face on the beach because of his weedy physique) and somehow I managed to buy spring chest expanders. I dedicated myself to his exercises and managed to increase my chest measurement but made little progress with other muscles. My summer hay fever also got worse. I got more interested in girls and in pursuit of this interest, joined a youth club in nearby Ystrad. This was run by a gentleman whom I think was more interested in boys. We went for long educational walks locally and danced a bit. I learnt to dance the waltz and the two-step just before the onset of rock and roll. By the time I reached sixteen, our music was totally overtaken by the Everly Brothers, Elvis and 'Rock Around the Clock' singer Bill Haley. My cousin David (from Rhiwmynach) was totally besotted by all of this; he was blessed with dark hair which he styled like Tony Curtis, attractive blue eyes and a dimple. He was very dedicated in his quest for the opposite sex and we often spent time in the deserted carriages at Devil's Bridge railway station, attempting to seduce local village girls.

We also went to local eisteddfodau to the same end. One night we went in David father's Austin Seven (David had already learnt to drive) to the King's Hall in Aberystwyth (now demolished) and happened to meet two attractive girls on the dodgems. Unbeknown to me at that time, one of these – Bethan – was later to become my wife. They were on holiday with their parents and were staying in an hotel on the prom. We had a whale of a time and were very late returning to Devil's Bridge!

Back home in the valley my best friend John

disappeared completely from school. The headmaster, fed up with his constant absences, had alerted his mother who hadn't been aware of what was happening. She decided to take him out of school and place him with Cardiff's David Morgan as a trainee manager in the drapery department. But this was not to be the end of our association. Although he eventually settled in England and became a producer with Jack de Manio on Radio 4's *Today* programme, we still kept in touch.

I spent the remainder of my time in the lower school with as little effort as was possible and faced the 'O' level exams with unjustified confidence, being rather expert at living in cloud-cuckoo land. I must have accidentally given all the right answers, because I passed all those I tried (except Latin, which I had dropped) including, amazingly, maths, at which you may remember I was no Einstein. This left the coast clear for me to join the sixth form if I could decide my subjects.

Since I was still keen on the white coat I opted for the three sciences: biology, chemistry and physics. My father was not too happy since he thought I was, if anything, an arts person. He was probably right. My mother was just happy that I was 'advancing'. It always reminds me of the legendary tale of the Rhondda Council member of the Education Committee. Annoyed at the chairman praising a candidate and his many qualifications, he suddenly got to his feet and exclaimed: 'These damn letters are all very nice, but wot I want to know is – do he 'ave 'is MATRIC (matriculation)?'

Well, there endeth lower school. On to the next chapter and higher…

CHAPTER 3

Higher and Lower

IT WAS AUTUMN, AND I began my period in the sixth form with enthusiasm, expectation and some trepidation – since I knew that my parents were relieved but hopeful. Carol was now embarking on her degree in Aberystwyth and my parents were confident that she would do well in her chosen arts subjects. They bought me the regulation white lab coat and, armed with this, I took my place in upper school.

Of the three science subjects, I much preferred biology under Mr Weaver; a serious individual but not without humour. My artistic talents could come to the fore in this subject and I produced masterpieces of anatomical art (akin to Damien Hirst's creations), much to the envy of other pupils and the amusement of Mr Weaver. I could also produce similar green extravaganzas in botany. We spent a lot of time in the laboratory dissecting mammals (rabbits and rats) as well as dogfish and frogs; simultaneously eating sandwiches without a qualm, drowned in the odour of formic acid. I was neat and tidy and all the labelling was immaculate. Weaver was pleased; that is, until the day I accidentally dropped a microscope which broke neatly in half. His complexion turned green and I don't think he ever subsequently viewed me in the same

53

light. Having said that, he continued to give me every attention.

Chemistry was the province of Mr Kiff, a large, bluff individual who enjoyed the occasional joke. I loved all the pipettes, retorts and chemicals. I particularly enjoyed open days when we as senior pupils could impress visitors with our often scant knowledge. I was a little fazed by all the chemical equations since they reminded me too much of maths. Nevertheless, I can still remember one of the longest names in organic compounds; I think it was: p-dimethylamino-benzal-rhodamine! We certainly loved the moment when Mr Kiff, intent on testing two new fume cupboards, set off some chemical compound producing thick smoke which the fans failed to disperse, resulting in the upper school being cleared for half a day. There were many bright pupils in this group who later became well-known doctors or chemists, though I was not destined to become one of these...

Physics (I have conveniently forgotten the teacher's name – well, it was over 50 years ago) became my Waterloo. It had not registered with me in lower school that there would be a great deal of mathematics in this subject at advanced level. I managed to struggle on (more in hope than in expectation) but physics was a definite low point in my timetable. Rather than draw attention to this, I soldiered on, ignorance being bliss.

At home in Eryl, my cousin Mary from Rhiwmynach lodged with us whilst attending Cardiff Art College, pending her finding cheap digs in the city. She stayed with us for a term, travelling by valley steam train from Ystrad to Cardiff General which was near the college. Her journey was very educational, since she was accompanied by other students who would become famous and be known as the 'Rhondda Painters'. Her presence at our home was also educational, since she was superb at drawing, portraiture and landscape; I was particularly drawn to her sketches from the 'life class' sessions at the college; but then I would be, wouldn't I? However, her lively presence came as a breath of fresh air, and since she was nearer Carol's age, they became good friends. Outside of school, I continued to play the organ in chapel, travel from cinema to cinema and play tennis with any girl in shorts.

I had some strange periods when I became dizzy in chapel (probably as a result of rapid growth) and thanks to the 'dying swan' trick, used this as a means of dodging services. I received much sympathy from my ever-attentive mother; father said nothing. During these periods, mornings would be spent reading in bed and evenings escaping to Maendy Mountain to contemplate the chapel from a safe distance. I became very keen on 35mm still photography at this time and took pictures of everything that moved (friends and relatives) and things that didn't (buildings, chapels and flowers); I became rather good at it and even began to process my own films. Although there was homework to do, it was not terribly high on my list of priorities, play being easier. But I must have done well enough to advance to second-year sixth. There, native intelligence was not sufficient nor any substitute for hard graft.

In this year, approaching the Higher exam, my parents decided to ease my path. They adapted the dining room into a sort of study for me to spread out my homework and SWOT! Chance would be a fine thing. Left to my own devices, I doodled and daydreamed, living in my own world of fantasy which was infinitely rewarding. This, coupled with the annual summer hay fever, made concentration difficult. I shall not make excuses. I had lived too long on my wits and background to succeed where others had worked and deserved success.

Although I had been successful in being accepted by colleges like Bristol, Nottingham and Aberystwyth prior to the results, I had not even entertained the idea that my eventual grades would exclude me. Meanwhile, in Aberystwyth, my sister was well on the way to becoming female president of the Union of Students. My parents (quite rightly) were thrilled with her success and devastated by my apparent failure.

Carol in presidential garb

My friend John, although still in the apprentice training in David Morgan's store, was approaching 18 and inevitably received his call-up papers from the government. National Service was still mandatory for all 18-year-olds and that would be my next prospect. I already had some notification, but because I was 'reading science' I was temporarily excused. The prospect of my 'going to war, or similar' was an imminent threat to my father, who hastily tried to get me into the establishments that would accept me. In the interim, he managed to get me into Cardiff Art College (would you believe) for a term, and I started a daily journey much as that taken previously by cousin Mary to that august establishment. Since I was naturally talented in that field and had sketches to prove it, I suddenly began an arts course – something of a *volte face*, and began to enjoy it. One day I was heavily criticised in life class, whose tutor thought I had shown too much imagination in portraying the model's breasts, portraying her more like Jayne Mansfield or Jane Russell than reality required.

Halfway through this term, I was suddenly thrown a lifeline: being accepted by Trinity College, Carmarthen because someone had dropped out. Trinity, at that time, was an educational college run by the Church and somewhat based on Oxbridge campuses, both in appearance and in style of tuition, with the college chapel taking pride of place. The principal was Dr Halliwell, a kindly northerner who was very sympathetic to the Welsh language. Teaching was based on small classes and even smaller tutorials. There were many leading members of Welsh cultural life who were lecturers there, including a certain Norah Isaac, who, although she was involved in drama, became a strong influence on my development.

My arrival there was to coincide for the first time that 'women' students were admitted to the college; my luck was in! So, here we go again, I thought, as I was bought the requisite college blazer, tie and striped scarf (essential in those formal days) and caught the train to my next educational establishment. How I wasn't even more dizzy in those days I shall never know.

Boys were billeted in the men's block and girls in a newly-built ladies' wing. I was quickly given a tutor and had to decide on my main subject. Since I was best qualified (if that's the expression) in science, I chose biology. The first general tutorial was interesting in that I met people with whom I would associate with for many years. Among these were Emyr Griffith (who would run the Wales Tourist Board and then A Taste of Wales) and Alun Cooper (a talented clarinettist who would run the Youth Training Schemes in Pembrokeshire). Another was John M O Jones, englynwr and one of the famous 'Bois y Cilie' family of poets. It was, at first glance, a highly civilised place and well grounded in the traditions of academia.

The late fifties were still times of discipline and comparatively good behaviour, unsullied by the more recent tendencies towards vandalism and rowdiness. My father, militant nonconformist though he was, was fairly content if I had any church influence in my life. I, on the other hand, though I played the chapel organ from time to time, was likely to miss more services than I attended.

The big change was to have one's own room. Tiny

Emyr Griffith and I act as bookends in this tutorial group

I was probably wondering where I could get a cup of coffee in this labratory session.

At the Trinity College organ

though it was, having only a bed, chairs and desk, it gave me my first real taste of *independence* and probably the stirrings of an awareness that I would have to plough my own furrow from now on. Along with the arrival of women in Trinity, there came the first moves toward bilingual tuition in higher education. If your speciality was in the arts, then you were offered (as far as possible) tuition in Welsh, but since I had opted for science and biology, the only medium was English. Even this would change within two years. The college students were mostly Welsh or English (there were no foreign students at that time) and many of the English had a church background. I instantly befriended Emyr Griffith and Alun Cooper, both from chapel backgrounds, because we got on well and had similar interests. But then, because the college was small, you got to know more or less everyone. Rugby star Dewi Bebb was my next-door neighbour.

During the week, lectures would be held during the day, coupled with required coursework in your room at night. There were only eight students in our lab which allowed for more detailed study than I had been used to. Wednesday afternoons were free for sport; in my case, free. We also socialised a great deal outside lectures. I naturally gravitated towards those studying drama: Mike Wright (who later became a BBC designer) and the much older George P Owen from Llangefni who was in his final year (having done National Service) and was destined to become drama producer in the BBC. So why I didn't opt for drama, I shall never know. Too careful I expect. Stick to what you know, boy!

It was then that I got to know Norah Isaac, an all-Welsh diminutive firebrand among the lecturers, a sort of Welsh Joan Littlewood. In spite of having stunted arms and knotted hands, she was the powerhouse in that department; her word was law. She was to be the driving influence on many who later found themselves in the BBC – John Hefin, who became BBC Wales Head of Drama, being one. Norah was a close friend and devout interpreter of the work of Wales' answer to the Bard, Saunders Lewis, whose work was not the easiest to stage. It was with the performance of one of his plays – *Amlyn ac Amig* – a grim tale, that I was to become 'entangled' with Norah. In the interim I ploughed on, getting involved in all aspects of student life, from Rags to late night revelling. There was music and there were girls. There were student summer balls and groping in the shrubbery. It was the age of experimentation and discovery. Halcyon days indeed!

This idyll continued into the following year when, in a moment of weakness, I was persuaded by Norah to perform, in my spare time, the part of Amlyn in her next production. She had been impressed by my voice and stature presumably, and I foolishly leaped at the chance. Of course I hadn't then quite realised the enormity of the role. Try memorising the telephone directory; this will give you some idea. But I was game and we commenced rehearsals.

During this particular year Carol, having graduated with honours galore from Aberystwyth, had begun to teach in Blaengarw secondary school and was already engaged to a fellow Aber student, Iolo from Barmouth who was studying for his doctorate. One day I received a letter from my mother saying that Carol had been home ill for some days. The following weekend, I caught the train home thinking I would jolly her up with news of my progress. On my arrival at Eryl, I was rather shocked at her condition. So, obviously, were my parents. She spent the weekend either in bed or on the toilet, where she visibly bled. I got the feeling that life in Blaengarw had been tough, and her diet in digs frugal. But she continued to smile and I spent most of the weekend at her bedside trying to raise her spirits before I had to return to college.

I continued my college activities, including the exertion of attempting to learn Saunders' verse, oblivious that my life would suddenly collapse. A fortnight later, I received a message from my mother that Carol had gone into the then East Glam Hospital for an operation for a colostomy (whatever that was), and could I perhaps call at the weekend to see her? On my return to Eryl, my mother was visibly distressed; my father, as usual, silent. We travelled to East Glam in Isaac Davies' car (a sympathetic deacon) and entered her ward. In spite of the fact that she was surrounded by tubes and the usual paraphernalia of post-op care, she looked well, smiled and was fairly animated. The relief was tangible...

Back in college, I attended lectures with renewed vigour until some three days later I was called out of one, given as I remember by Bobi Jones, giant among modern Welsh poets, since the principal wanted to see me. I scurried along the corridors towards the ante-chapel without thinking that I was about to face a seminal moment in my life. I was greeted by the kindly, grey-suited Dr Halliwell who proffered his hand, saying, without preamble: 'I'm sorry to have to say that your sister has just died.' I must have turned white and staggered on my feet at this unexpected bombshell, because the good doctor quickly pulled forward a convenient chair and thrust a glass of water into my numb fingers. 'I'm very sorry,' he said, 'I hadn't realised that this was unexpected.'

Not only was it unexpected, I had never even contemplated such an event. He immediately called a senior student, who led me back to my quarters. I sat there in silence, deeply traumatised until someone arrived to say that a relative would call to transport me to Ton and, presumably, whatever Hell lay in store. In the interim, friends called to offer their condolences which fell on deaf ears. My mind was already in Ton.

After a wordless journey back via Llandeilo, the Beacons, Hirwaun and Rhigos we arrived at an Eryl with its curtains unfamiliarly drawn. Entering through the back door I could already hear my mother's tears. She was alone in the kitchen. We hugged each other, tears flowed, but little was said. My father was in his usual chair in the study being comforted by his long-term friend Ivor (the undertaker), also weeping. My father stared at me through red eyes, almost in disbelief, as if he couldn't grasp the fact that I was still there. I retreated to the kitchen and tried to comfort my inconsolable mother. Later it emerged that Carol had suffered a haemorrhage (occasioned, so my mother said, by her bandages being too tight) and that she accused the hospital of negligence. She was to maintain this view until her own death; but her heart was already broken.

I do not intend to recount in detail the horrors that the next days brought; it would be infinitely too depressing for the reader and not the function of this memoir. All I will say is that any faith we had was severely tested as we faced the very public service in Jerusalem before an equally massive and public committal in Aberaeron and Llanddewi Aberarth Church. All Carol's relatives and college friends turned up to mourn her passing. I shall only mention one particular traumatic moment: when Aunty Elaine asked me to view the body (as was common practice then) which I reluctantly did. How could such a lovely, lively, always smiling, intelligent girl become a white and still object? Her lips were the greatest shock; under the pallor they were blue. Later my father, in one of his poems, quoted CA Trypanis who called them 'the blue anemone of Death'. He was right and the image has never left me.

Following these ghastly events, I returned to Trinity and the prospect of life having to continue for me at least. As for my parents, I knew my father would sublimate his grief in his books and writings; my mother had no such release and would spend the rest of her life in mourning. My fellow students were very understanding and sensibly, scarcely mentioned the event. Norah Isaac, on the other hand, was deeply troubled. She saw that I had not only lost weight but also needed swift attention. Let's face it, I had accepted the lead role in her next epic production. She began force-feeding me every evening in her room: fruit juices and a pick-up concoction called 'Froment' full of goodness and yeast. She simultaneously coached me in the Saunders play whilst I recovered slowly. Fortunately, I have a sort of photographic memory which enables me to not so much memorise, as *visualize* or recall individual pages. This was the only way in which I could retain the pages of blank verse that the part of Amlyn demanded.

When the time came for the performances I was

word perfect, ready to face an audience of many literary luminaries whom Norah had invited. Emyr, who played the bed-bound Amig, had the distinct advantage of being able to secrete his script under the bedclothes! The play was a huge success; so much so, that we performed excerpts from it for TWW in their then Pontcanna studios. This taste of television and its associated paraphernalia did much to arouse my interest in the media, but this desire to be involved didn't come to fruition for a few more years.

Around this time my father was busy achieving great success in the National Eisteddfod, being crowned in Rhos in 1961 for a poem on Dylan Thomas.

Back in Trinity, exams came to the fore and somehow I managed to graduate with distinction. At that time, moves were afoot to amalgamate the college with the

Amlyn ac Amig, TWW 1960

My father winning the crown in the Dyffryn Maelor Eisteddfod, 1961

University of Wales at Aberystwyth. This being so, I got the chance to spend time in Aber during a third year. No sooner than I had begun to enjoy life there, than there came another call from Trinity. They had been contacted by Mr James, headmaster of Ysgol Dewi Sant, the secondary school serving North Pembrokeshire. He urgently needed a teacher of biology and general science in the lower and middle school; preferably, in the new climate of increasing use of Welsh, one who could speak the language. My name had been mentioned, so with some trepidation, I caught a bus to St David's on my next pilgrimage.

The school was fairly small and sited a little distance from the city on the Haverfordwest road. The headmaster, Mr James (whom I later discovered was known as 'Tojo' because of his tall but oriental appearance), took me in his gown for a tour of the school. He was charming and enquired a lot of my background, together with my interest in drama. I later found that there was a thriving theatre group called Theatr Dewi Sant in the school run by the deputy head, Islwyn Thomas from Fishguard. To cut a long story short, much to my parents' bemusement, I accepted his offer to join the staff the following term at the princely salary of £39 a month. In the meantime, I spent some weeks in Llangrannog Urdd camp, supervising children as a 'swog'. There I continued my interest in film, producing a short documentary of some forty minutes on life in the then tented and slightly impermanent camp. This must be archival now and I must still have it somewhere! Llangrannog is now a thriving youth centre with all modern facilities. Then, we all mucked in doing every conceivable task, but the spirit was great – and so were some of the other (female) swogs.

Still bitten by the media bug, I continued to respond to adverts I saw in the paper. The best from the BBC was the mention of there being a need for an aerial rigger in Northern Scotland, but since I suffered vertigo this hadn't appealed much...

Soon, the time came for the move west. It was suggested that I stayed with a Mrs Hern in New Street, a robin-like, Welsh-speaking widow and member of Tabernacle Methodist Chapel, who kept lodgers. She already had a bank clerk and had room for more. And so it was that I became a member of whatever sort of society that existed in that very remote corner of Wales. Still being car-less, it took me some considerable time to get my bearings. The school was a 12-minute walk away, but felt more like half an hour in the rain and gales that often blasted this particular corner of the country. There were, unsurprisingly, few trees, just stunted and bent shrubs in the hedgerows. But when it was fine, the skies were an azure blue that I had never experienced in the valley of my youth.

The schoolchildren were charming and largely well behaved; most were from farming stock. They were attentive and keen, at least until the age of fifteen when many were more interested in returning to the farm. Understandably, the girls were more keen to get on, always occupying the front rows in class. I felt almost threatened by their interest. The other staff members were also supportive and made me very welcome. But what was a young man to do after school hours, especially in winter when beaches were too cold? There were generally a few answers to this. I started to re-attend chapel, not from any particular conviction but because of the potential for company. There was a nice organ in the Tabernacle and I was soon on the rota. Secondly, there was the new minister, Haydn Thomas and his pretty wife Doreen, slightly older than I but young enough to be fun. I spent many nights in their manse, having supper or playing table tennis. Just as well, because the fare in my digs was, shall we say, frugal.

The other family I befriended were John Evans and his elderly parents who lived in Naw Ffynnon near Solva. They also went to chapel, his father being a deacon. But you would find no family less grey or inhibited than they. They were archetypical North Pembs types with a razor-like humour, a hunger for gossip and a talent for mimicry unsurpassed. There was Mr Evans senior, with arthritis-ridden hands and a twinkle in his blue eyes, Mrs Evans, diminutive brown, with an infectious giggle and their son John, with an earnest expression which belied a comic talent. We had tremendous fun (and meals) in Delfryn and I used to take the cine camera along to make short mute films of our exploits – much to their eventual amusement. Oh, happy days! I nearly forgot how serious life could be...

John drove a car (which was useful in our exploration of the area) since he taught in a primary school in the east of the county. He was also involved in Theatr Dewi Sant, often playing villains or severe characters not a bit like himself. These friends made life easier to bear than it otherwise might have been in my early twenties. I had the odd 'liaison', much to the amusement of the Evans family. Nothing which could be deemed serious, but enough to engage me with the opposite sex and to

An ageing Archbishop in *St Joan*, 1961

cherish the odd magic moment on the Preseli outcrops. I even remember saving the odd pound from my small salary in order to catch a bus to Haverfordwest and buy a green jacket, matching tie and (ugh!) drip-dry polyester shirt, in order to impress someone. Pathetic! Fine weather gave me the chance to explore nearby beaches like Caerfai or White Sands with Haydn and Doreen, and I grew to love the landscape and its people. I would make use of this knowledge later in my career.

In school we performed Shaw's *Saint Joan* in which I played a very tall archbishop. It was produced by the intelligent and dynamic Islwyn Thomas with, as I recall, the esteemed writer DJ Williams in the audience.

Meanwhile, I continued to apply for media jobs (more in hope than expectation) until an interesting one caught my attention:

'Wanted: an assistant floor manager in Cardiff to assist with the preparation of programmes, rehearsals and performance...'

Not having the slightest idea of what the job involved, I sent an application, quoting Norah Isaac as one of my referees. Amazingly, I got a letter within a month asking me to come for interview. Gosh! This would mean having to alert the head. He, surprisingly, was unfazed by this news. 'I didn't think we'd keep you long – I don't think your heart is in teaching'. He knew all right.

I caught the required buses and trains home to gather strength to face (or bluff) my way through the expected interview on the following Monday. My parents, alone and sad though they were, tried to be encouraging, although they had little notion of what I was attempting. Monday dawned and I caught the (by now) diesel train to Cardiff's Queen Street station and took the short walk to Park Place and the HQ of the BBC in Wales. I had often seen the building and its winking valves and red lights from the valley train and had always been intrigued by what exactly lay within.

Nervously approaching the interview in my best tweed jacket and tie bought in Haverfordwest

I had not long to wait in what seemed an ordinary Victorian building – typical of Cardiff – before I was ushered up some plush carpeted stairs to the interview room overlooking the Civic Centre buildings.

Now this is significant. Even though I was trying for a lowly job in the burgeoning TV industry, I was faced by a phalanx of senior staff: Alun Oldfield Davies, Controller; Hywel Davies, Head of Programmes; Aneirin Talfan Davies, Deputy; and another I can't remember but who was very important. In those days, they really cared who joined the Beeb. The interview was kindly, but probing. I can't now remember what was asked or said; I think Norah got a mention. Half an hour passed in a blur and I was out in Park Place again. I returned, none the wiser, to St David's and school.

Within a month I received a BBC envelope through the post informing me that I was being offered a six-month trial – take it or leave it. I went to see the head again. He was very positive. 'Give it a go' was his advice. Was he glad to get rid of me, one wondered? I took his advice and said farewell to my newfound and dear friends. Three of my 'O' level pupils, all girls, gave me a book on film and wept suitably copious tears. One of them was Ruth Barker, who has since become one of the county's premier folk singers. I would meet her again, on location, in other circumstances. Life's great adventure began again in earnest.

CHAPTER 4

Into the Arms of Aerial

IT WAS 1961 AND I was about to make my biggest career move yet. I was going to forget any science I ever thought I knew and become a media person; to prove finally to myself that there was 'no business like show business'. Of course, I was later to learn that any number of BBC staff had made some impossible leap – from reading law to set designer, from preacher to producer, from linguist to director – the list is endless. I was not that unique. I arrived at Park Place HQ to chat with TRJ Williams (Tom Stick), a short, beaming, urbane head of the admin staff, who explained the nature of my contract, took many personal details and told me to report to 'Broadway' and to trail an established assistant floor manager (AFM), a certain Dafydd Peate, so that I could 'learn the ropes'. If I was being sent to Broadway then I was surely on the road to showbiz! Broadway, in fact, turned out to be a cluster of terraced houses and old chapel buildings between Sapphire Street and Clifton Street off the rather seedy Newport Road. It no longer exists and there are now new houses on the site.

Broadway's entrance (via Sapphire Street) was fronted by a small BBC TV sign and commissionaire's desk manned by Tom, an uncle-like figure in full uniform who was eventually superseded by Charles, a younger, taller and less obsequious type. I was checked in by Tom (security was not the serious business it has become today) and shown to studio A scene dock to meet my mentor. At that time Broadway consisted of a large scene dock (accessed through roller doors from Clifton St.), associated prop room, single camera and news desk, studio A (the converted chapel) and engineering stores, make-up and wardrobe, a smaller studio B, and a canteen upstairs. A virtual Hollywood in my eyes!

I met Dafydd, a tall, dark, rather slim young man, wearing headphones (or 'cans') around his neck. He greeted me in Welsh. I later understood that he was the only son of Dr Iorwerth Cyfeiliog Peate who had established the Welsh Folk Museum (now the Museum of Welsh Life) in St Fagans. Bright and intelligent though he was, Dafydd had failed in his first year at university, had travelled to Paris to work at pavement cafes (where he got a taste for black coffee and Gaulois fags) before having to do National Service; opting for humping corpses in a hospital morgue. He was hard all right! Having said that, he turned out to be a good and willing teacher as he explained the mysteries of studio A; the cameras, the monitors, the vision gallery and the sound boom. We became good friends, and I would find myself principal speaker at his untimely funeral. But then, it was all enthusiasm and discovery. I told him I was still having to travel daily from the valley and he suggested that we shared rented accommodation he had found in Cathedral Road. I leapt at this chance for total independence and we jointly agreed to the contract. The ground floor of a large Victorian house was too good to miss.

We moved in with just beds as I remember, but eventually made ourselves fairly comfortable, except that the road (being on a level with the Taff) was notoriously damp before the days of the Cardiff Barrage. We couldn't afford to heat it much. It was, however, an ideal 'pad' for parties – of which we held many! In fact, as I discovered, Dafydd was totally dedicated to late night wandering and the pursuit of 'birds' of any hue, age or inclination, and would spend nights down in Dockland bent on seduction. I quickly discovered that I couldn't keep up, so Dafydd became an absent friend for much of the time, although still managing to do his job efficiently. What energy! We often went on the weekend to his parents' place in St Fagans and shot rabbits and pigeons in the forest grounds with 12-bores. We were both similarly privileged, having been raised in homes where books, art and poetry were revered. Although my father and Dr Peate were always at loggerheads through correspondence in Welsh newspapers, my friendship with Dafydd was to last through his marriage in Pennant to his premature death.

Within weeks I ceased 'trailing' in studio and began to enter the schedule to operate on my own along with some six other AFMs, most of whom ended up as directors or producers. In those days, the BBC believed in grooming their staff from ground level; now, I'm afraid they seem to get producers off the street with little or no experience. The advantage for us was that we were given experience in most aspects of TV work, so that in later years no one could pull the wool over our eyes. I certainly worked with some interesting characters:

Evelyn Williams, a tall, elegant woman, dripping with jewellery, produced children's programmes, specializing in puppets; Ivor Rees (former minister and poet) produced light entertainment together with Jack Williams (a former theatre designer), who introduced revue-type programmes and sketches. Others were involved in news and sport. You had to adapt your style (or *modus operandi*) according to the producer, but generally I got on with them all and was rarely chastised. These were good days and we spent much time in the canteen exchanging gossip and discussing the potential of jobs being advertised.

It was, in the early 60s, a time of great expansion in television. The innovative Hugh Carlton-Greene was running the BBC network in London and exciting changes were in store. There would be more purpose-built buildings, bigger budgets, more scintillating programmes and, what was most important to us, more JOBS! It was during this period that I started occasionally attending Crwys Road Methodist Chapel where my uncle Albert (who had been head of the Board of Health in Cardiff) had been deacon. I went with a view to recce the talent there – naturally. One night I was surprised to see a familiar face in the gallery, a face I had last seen in the King's Hall in Aberystwyth on the bumper cars. It was Bethan Pierce and her younger sister, Siân. Our eyes met, she smiled in recognition and I'm afraid that all was lost from then on – marriage was inevitable. It took a little time, but more of that later...

I promised not to bore you and this is in no way a formal history of television in Wales, rather a general impression. I am only noting the names of those who impinged on my development; indeed, some dates are probably suspect. Luckily for me, all areas of Welsh television were developing in the early 60s, including drama production. This was led by DJ Thomas (a quiet, academic, bespectacled gentleman from Swansea) who tended to favour the classic plays; then Dafydd Gruffydd (son of the great Welsh writer WJ Gruffydd) who was dapper, debonair, had an eye for the ladies and generally sported a tan, since he had a villa on the island of Gozo. He favoured more action and thrills. They ensured that Wales would be recognised for its drama productions and often obtained good UK network slots for them. Their plays were performed live or 'as live' to a VTR machine in Bristol. Any film was usually limited to opening titles, also run in from a remote telecine machine.

I very much enjoyed rehearsals, which were normally held in a convenient church hall. There, the floor would be marked out by the AFM in sticky tape to define the shape, borders, doors, etc. of the eventual studio set. We would also get bits of old furniture and cheap props to enable actors to familiarise themselves with using them while playing their parts. These were generally provided by Jack, the prop master in Broadway. Location work was virtually non-existent when I started – except for the filmed titles that is. The director was occasionally Artie (Arthur Williams), an old, lugubrious, theatrical type with pimples and a sonorous voice. What I enjoyed most (apart from being prompter) was to act as stand-in for various characters who couldn't make it to rehearsal. Dafydd was very amused by my caricatures of these artists, but he was always encouraging. I met well-known stars in this work: the Houston brothers (Donald and Glyn), Stanley Baker, Rachel Thomas, and a host too numerous to mention here. In general, I found them very pleasant and a joy to work with.

After final complete technical runs and costume fittings, the whole circus landed in studio A for the recording (or live transmission) where the complete drama would be played out in 'real time' – hoping that cameras wouldn't come into shot and nobody broke a leg tripping on a cable as he or she ran from set to set. This was normality in those days and any mistakes and false entrances were frowned upon, since editing was expensive, around £40 per edit as I recall. (Drama crews today have got it easy with single camera and multiple edits.) As AFMs, we not only had a script in hand to prompt but also a button to press so that the unfortunate viewer didn't *hear* the prompter. As you can imagine, these recording days were fraught with tension and when we finished, everybody departed with relief to the BBC club (set up in a house in Newport Road) where we could drink and, hopefully, recover. One advantage to working like this was that you learnt quickly; if you didn't, then you never got beyond the trial period. This all made for a sort of camaraderie among crew members which never left us.

My own trial period had now ended and I was called to TRJ's office to be told that I could join the permanent staff. At last, a bona fide BBC man! In general, this position was not abused by staff (who might have rested on their oars or over-fiddled expenses); we were too busy trying to clamber up through the system to jeopardise any progress. There were some drones, as there are in any company, but they were generally known and didn't progress very far. Since the big expansion of BBC Wales had not yet occurred, we were all on first name terms and gossip travelled fast.

During this time, Dafydd and I occasionally travelled to London to visit the new TV Centre or Lime Grove or other seedy establishments. In the centre we would sometimes watch a sitcom being recorded or mix with well-known faces in the bar like Steptoe, Morecombe and Wise or the actors playing *The Good Life*. This all inspired us to move further up the ladder. Shows like *That Was The Week That Was* found us all watching avidly in the Newport Road club. It had a huge audience; important debates were even rescheduled in parliament so that MPs could watch it – all in monochrome of course. Colour TV was yet to start...

In Wales, talents like Ryan and Ronnie began to emerge, courtesy of a light entertainment programme called *Studio B* recorded in Broadway. Suddenly, television began to show its potential as a medium in which staff and artistes could actually make a living. In a word, it became more professional, as well as respectable, even to those who thought theatre was God.

ODE TO A MONOCHROME PAST AND A COLOURED FUTURE

Is it not strange
How halcyon days are viewed
In monochrome?
How 'Golden Years'
We oft recall,

Those 'days of yore'
Are lost
For evermore
When programmes made
For programmes' sake
Were launched into the ether,
When money-men were yet unborn
And 'vision' ruled from dusk to dawn
When forms and calculators
Never figured
In our quest.
But, I'll be jiggered,
Now
We sit and wait
As money-men deliberate
And call the shots.
Though 'coloured' now,
Our screens are filled
With dirty brown
And green,
The tarnished coin
And dirty notes
Of money-men
Supreme!

(RL Private poems)

I don't intend listing all our productions here, but there were many highly successful ones; so much so, that well-known network producers such as Sidney Newman brought their productions (and female stars we all fancied) to studio A. I managed to work quite closely with some of these producers since I had begun vision-mixing dramas. This would put me at some slight advantage when trying for directors' posts later on. One of the directors was James MacTaggart, who now has a BAFTA Award named in his honour. We also had freelance drama producers (like Emyr Humphries and Wilbert Lloyd-Roberts) who frequently rehearsed in North Wales but recorded in Broadway.

At around this time the BBC revealed that the grounds of former Baynton House mansion were being developed in Llandaff as a broadcasting centre for radio and television. This was the brainchild of Controller Alun Oldfield Davies, who would still be controller when it was completed. Furthermore, offices were earmarked for production in the General Accident Building (presumably not meant as a joke) in Newport Road. Finally, a deserted chapel in nearby Stacey Road was being adapted as a news studio with newsroom and offices on the ground floor. For the staff, this was all very heartening news. Although some of the expansion would involve the appointment of people from the outside, we on the inside hoped we might get 'first bite of the cake'. We were all like jockeys about to start the Derby. In my spare time I continued to 'act' and joined the BBC Players.

Although I was content with my lot and had increased responsibilities, I was aware that I had to be in the job race. Eventually, large adverts began to appear internally and in the press, ranging from researchers to stage managers, from directors to producers, all a sign of the huge boom in the burgeoning television industry. Plans were made to re-name the Beeb in Wales to BBC Wales in 1964 and transfer it to Channel

Monday, 25th March 1963

7.30 p.m. B.B.C. PLAYERS
THE DAY OF THE MARCH by Tom Richards

Cast in order of appearance:

Gabriel Foster (the Innkeeper)	Ray Brace
Meg (his daughter)	Ann Clwyd Lewis
Mabel (his wife)	Nest Williams
Alex Selkirk (a journalist)	Paul Sproxton
P.C. Bryn Owen	Geraint Stanley Jones
P.C. Stan Barnett	Peter Granger
Toby Cartland (A gentleman farmer)	Joe Payne
The Rev. Pedrog Price	William Aaron
Alun Jenkins	Richard Lewis
Dai Lewis (a butcher)	Brydan Griffiths
County Councillor Joe Williams	Hywel Owen
Vladimir Joneski	Emyr Jenkins
Sir Wulfnoth Godwin	Arthur Williams
Miss Prunella Brown	Margaret Glenys Jones
Mrs. Louella Deacon Marvon	Enyd Williams

Other parts played by members of the B.B.C. Club.

Stage Managers: Mike Painter, Peter Hook, Alison Fear, Peter Fear
Lighting: Peter Granger
Design: Colin Shaw
Produced by: Colin Shaw, George Owen

Scene: The bar of the Angler's Elbow, an Inn on the England-Wales border. The time is the present.

Act I   A Sunday.
Act II   The same—the following day.
Act III The same—the following Sunday.

The border line between England and Wales runs through the middle of the bar of the Angler's Elbow. It also runs through the middle of the lives of some of the characters. The Welshmen who come there are fugitives from the dry Welsh Sunday. One of them, through no fault of his own, also becomes somewhat of a fugitive from the embraces of the two World Powers, Russia and America. The Boundaries Commission is also interested in the somewhat curious shape of the border at this point. The border is, in fact, even odder than it seems and the very Inn itself, with the land around it, becomes an object of even more intense interest to the two foreign Powers.

At the conclusion of the Play, the Adjudicator will address the Company and the audience.

Musical selections will be played at each performance throughout the week by
THE CARDIFF MUNICIPAL MUSICAL SOCIETY

I struggled with unfamiliar guitar chords fortified with drinks from Nest Owen (announcer) and Ray Brace (AFM) from behind the bar

13. We all remember Derek Trimby's adverts for the new channel and the catchy jingle. So there we were, applying for every job in sight, almost confident that we would all get something! I was eventually called for interview – yet again to Park Place.

There sat the usual half a dozen familiar senior staff (not as senior as those for my AFM interview – a sign of the times), including a comparatively new face, Alan Protheroe, former industrial correspondent who was the newly appointed News Editor. I was in fact being considered for the post of News Director! I had begun to stumble my way through the questions being asked by the others when I heard a military band outside. Alan immediately asked me: 'That band outside, is *that* news?' I thought quickly and answered without hesitation, 'Well it *might* be. Royalty could be here, or war have been declared; I would have to check with the barracks...' This may have not been the answer expected, but Alan smiled his usual rather toothless grin and I was offered the job there and then.

Suddenly, I was a DIRECTOR. Any plans I had for drama would have to be on the backburner for some time since I was now a NEWSMAN. I had never even imagined this and would have to learn from scratch. So I eventually joined that strange gang called the newsroom in Stacey. The editor of course was Alan, who spoke with a posh voice (similar to that of programme head Hywel Davies on whom he had modelled himself) which sometimes lapsed into a western valleys slang. He would later become Assistant Director General in London. The deputy was Wynford Jones (with a florid complexion and permanent pipe) and the chief assistant Tudor Phillips from the *Aberdare Leader* – all were Welsh

The proud owner of a BBC ID card

speaking. Among the performers or reporters would be Brian Hoey, John Darran, Jeffrey Iverson, David Parry Jones and cricketer Peter Walker. Another director who had been appointed was Gareth Wyn Jones, who would hold the fort with the new flagship *Wales Today* until I was released from other duties. I can't remember the salary but it was considerably more than being an AFM. I could now begin to plan my future with more confidence...

As soon as I arrived at Stacey Road, I recommenced my pursuit of Bethan, who was in Bangor Uni studying French. I had been bowled over by her ready smile, hazel eyes and dark curly hair and was determined to make contact. One day, I spoke to Geraint Morris (who had just become an AFM and would eventually direct *Z-Cars*, *Softly, Softly* and *The Onedin Line*) who amazingly had been in Bangor with her and knew her telephone number! Although she had been in France (near Chartres) for a year as part of her course, she was now in hostel digs in Chateau Rhianfa, a Victorian castellated pile on the Anglesey side of the Menai Strait. She would be in Cardiff on the weekend and we arranged to meet in a pub in town. After that, we never looked back. I soon met her parents who lived in Insole Place, Llandaff. Her father (who reminded me of Cary Grant) had a permanent tan and was in the wholesale dairy business; her mother (of farming stock with incredibly blue eyes) wore the trousers, and was from Talybont in Cardiganshire. I think I was accepted,

Bethan at Bangor University

because the affair forged ahead. I would send her letters to Bangor every week (in a BBC TV envelope) filled with love poems filched from recognised poets, all stating my undying love.

One of our news assistants was David Morris Jones. He had also been to Bangor Uni and had lived in Beaumaris, which he visited every other week. Gratefully, I would hitch a lift with him in his car (at much peril to life and limb); he would drop me off at Chateau Rhianfa and pick me up on his way back to Cardiff. One day, on the occasion of the Bangor Uni Ball, Bethan and I arrived at the Trearddur Bay Hotel to join a strangely silent crowd around the communal television set in the foyer. President Kennedy had just been assassinated! It certainly put a dampener on that particular evening, but fortunately not on our relationship, which continued to grow.

Back at Stacey Road the new programme *Wales Today* established itself and became immensely popular with the viewers. Having been in drama (with its rehearsal and detailed preparation) I hadn't realised just how hectic news programmes could be. It all seemed to be last minute, done on the trot, subject to constant change; all the activity compressed into an hour before the programme and the transmission itself. Although I pressed for more time, nobody paid much attention. I was up and down that staircase to the studio like a hamster on a wheel. I trust it made me fit, but the sheer stress wasn't to my benefit. Once I arrived, Gareth Wyn would tend to rush off on some 'safari' or other, chasing this or that story. He once went to Borneo and Sarawak following the Welsh Regiment (when he and Brian Hoey had to be contacted by Alan, via the Foreign

Office, in an attempt to secure their return) and in the interim I tried to hold the fort. I didn't mind. It was good experience and Gareth was only doing what I would have done, had I been given the opportunity.

At the helm I met all sorts who were 'in town tonight': Tom Jones, Eric Sykes, Sean Connery, Shirley Bassey. This state of affairs continued until we got a new trainee, Philip Chilvers, pupil of John Chilvers of Swansea Grand Theatre fame. He was enthusiastic and learnt quickly, giving me the means to escape the daily grind. I could now go on outside broadcasts (OBs), cover elections and chase major stories. Among these, memorably, was when Gwynfor Evans was elected in Carmarthen and the local chief constable led the singing. My coverage was given a network screening and is now archival. Another was the investiture of Prince Charles in Caernarfon; a major broadcasting event in the UK where I shared a room with Raymond Baxter and others. I acted as local Welsh-speaking liaison officer to UK reporters. This was all 'dramatic' to say the least, especially when reporter Martin Bell (later white-suited independent MP) and I chased after an explosion which occurred in a railway siding as the royal coach was approaching the castle. I also remember the nights spent in the Royal Hotel observing the excesses of Princess Margaret and Lord Snowdon as they publicly drank the night away. We interviewed the good lord on the castle parapet but had to edit his somewhat strong language. These were certainly interesting times.

During this 'news' period of my life in broadcasting I was to have several different 'pads' in the city. The Cathedral Road flat became too expensive to maintain, so Dafydd and I amicably went our separate ways.

He was already energetically chasing a radio studio manager, Eirlys, a stunning brunette from Pennant in Cardiganshire, and they would eventually marry. I left the flat, considerably more worldly-wise but exhausted. I then met Hugh Williams (another former biologist) from Cardigan, a graduate who resembled Peter Sellers and was a trainee director in BBC Wales. He was dossing (I think that's an appropriate description) in Stacey Road. These rooms were being let by Ernie (of European origin with fractured English), who was an inspector on Cardiff buses. I was given a tiny garret room and shared a bathroom and kitchen with whoever happened to be in the house. Ernie was very welcoming, particularly to ladies who were looking for company. The ebb and flow of bodies up and down his stairs was very educational.

The house froze in winter and I always remember attempting to wake Hugh one morning (he likes his bed) only to find about two inches of snow on his counterpane which had blown in through the broken windowpane. We became firm pals; so much so that he would eventually be best man at my wedding. He didn't last long in the Beeb, especially after he was locked into a country estate by an irate landowner who objected to his filming (without permission) and demanded a ransom from the Head of Programmes, Aneirin Talfan Davies. After this, Hugh 'went to Coventry' (in all senses of the phrase) to resume academic life as a lecturer in Media Studies. As they say, 'If you can't do it – teach it!' He eventually ended up as Dean of the Faculty of Education at Warwick University. Currently, he is in retirement, overlooking the sea from his plush flat in Bournemouth...

Now I had to find alternative accommodation. This was offered by two colleagues: Artie Williams (whom I'd met directing drama) and a short, noisy individual called Islwyn Maelor Evans, a floor manager from the Wrexham area. What Islwyn lacked in inches, he made up in character, having a deep, resonant, 'actor's voice' and a wild personality to match. They were like Bootsie and Snudge together, and very funny. Their flat was in Newport Road, near the funeral home roundabout. It was to this location that I would stagger back from my 'stag night'...

The wedding wasn't long in coming, as Bethan and I prepared for the big event. We had secured rooms temporarily in Llandaff Road pending the completion of a cluster of modern houses in The Green, Radyr. From among the twenty houses being built there, we had chosen number 7 which was semi-detached, priced at £4,250. We couldn't afford the £4,500 charged for the detached variety.

The wedding was held on 19 September 1964 at Crwys Road. The reception at the Park Hotel would be a 'dry affair' at my father's insistence, although, with so many Beeb types on the guest list, there would be no guarantee it would continue in this vein! In fact, I can still visualise Alan Protheroe passing bottles under the table to his staff...

We left for our honeymoon in a tiny blue Austin car which we had jointly purchased and headed for Ireland, via Fishguard Harbour. There, we left the car (which only just made it) because we had hired a Morris Minor for our trip around the emerald isle. On the rather tatty, ageing ferry to Cork we consummated our marriage, carrying on with activity that had started

Hugh Williams (best man), Geraint Morris and Alun Cooper (ushers) and David Lloyd occupy the back row

that summer in Aunty Lilian's house, Llys Cynfelin, in Taliesin. There she had indulged us by being absent most of the time while we spent a long hot fortnight in and around Cors Fochno and Borth beach. As a spinster (although she'd had a torrid affair with academic and poet TH Parry-Williams before his marriage, in spite of being twice his height) she had been very beautiful, had known many suitors and understood that lovers are best left alone.

In Ireland we drove in leisurely fashion around the southern coast to Killarney, Galway and onward to the unique Connemara peninsula enjoying every Irish mile. We then advanced to Dublin where we had booked rooms in the Jury Hotel. It was here that I had the first demonstration of my new wife's determination and strength of character. The rooms offered were not to the standard we had expected and Bethan went down and remonstrated with the manager, whereas I would have probably meekly accepted things. We were instantly transferred to a new wing with 5-star rating. How we enjoyed those three days, mostly spent in bed, but we also managed to squeeze in an Abbey Theatre production, *The Plough and the Stars* I think it was!

On our return to Wales, the Radyr house was still unfinished and we suffered the cramped flat (now with accompanying cat Pws and smelly litter tray) until it was ready. This involved several stand-up rows between the redoubtable Bethan and the harassed builder. Yours truly kept out of it. I was, however, worried that I still wasn't being particularly creative, and the newsroom began to look more like the doldrums. Inevitably, there would shortly be a family to look after. I was jolted out of this reverie shortly after we moved to The Green.

I was sitting having a sandwich in the newsroom when a call came from a Merthyr reporter. He said, 'There's been a mud-slide in Aberfan – I hear there are some children involved at a school there.' This simple message began the busiest period the BBC Wales newsroom had ever seen. Within a day, most networks in the world had sent reporters to Cardiff. From Hong Kong to the USA they arrived, together with their film crews. The magnitude of the Aberfan disaster suddenly hit us. All the big network reporters were coming. The Queen herself would visit. All day long we sent studio bulletins to the network from our small studio, the first being read by Ronnie Williams (of Ryan and Ronnie), who also did duty news reading. We could scarcely cope with the influx of work and people. As the facts emerged of the full horror of this disaster, I found myself in the stricken village seeing the 'slurry', volunteer digging teams, and bodies laid out in the temporary morgue in Aberfan chapel. I had initially telephoned Bethan to say I wouldn't be home that night and would be sleeping in the newsroom. As it transpired, it was more like three nights. Anyone who was involved with this tragedy will never forget it… I certainly will not.

Following these fateful events, I was eventually given the chance to have a change and take a break from hard newsgathering. The magazine programme *Heddiw* was the Welsh language flagship on BBC Wales and more directors were needed. I went on attachment there. John Roberts Williams was editor, others being Geraint Stanley Jones (the producer who later became Head of Programmes, then Controller, then Chief Executive of S4C), Deryk Williams (who also joined S4C as Head of Programmes), together with others who would eventually lead Welsh language television. The programme was fronted by Owen Edwards, who would also eventually become Controller BBC Wales, and then launch the S4C service as First Executive. There were many other reporters or directors who would become leading names among those who ran the Welsh television service.

In the programmes office in 'General Accident' I was instantly made welcome and soon realised that although *Heddiw* was a daily live programme, the emphasis was less on hard news and more on entertainment. Although it had a newsreader and did many contemporary news stories (usually in studio), it had greater emphasis on magazine items gathered on film. That suited me because of my early experiences with the medium and because I had directed several film stories for *Wales Today*. *Heddiw's* style meant there was much greater potential for imaginative use of film. Our pattern of working spanned three weeks at a time: a preparation week, when local newspapers and stories were scanned and assessed and a schedule of filming drawn up; a filming week, usually away somewhere in the wilds of Wales, when the material for six or more mini-films was gathered; then an editing week to finalize the packages for transmission the following week. This schedule was an excellent opportunity for me to be organised, to ensure that I had a full week of shooting (sometimes two stories a day, separated by miles of travelling) and that I could be demonstrably creative.

Some of the other directors were not as keen to have a full schedule. So began a year or two when I was constantly on the go, and Bethan did some French

Trying out the presenter's chair in studio

Dafydd Peate, Rhys Lewis, R Alun Evans, Arwel Ellis Owen, yours truly and Robin Jones

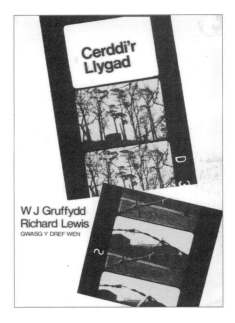

teaching in Radyr as we awaited Elen, our first child. Straight away I became quite popular with film crews, not just because I was quite knowledgeable about film technique but mainly because they liked a *full schedule*. I was instantly drawn to cameraman Barrie Thomas and his sound recordist Tomi from Fishguard since Barrie was very creative, an artist in his own right, who would eventually retire to run an antique shop in the town. He was also a silversmith and specialized in the restoration of antique guns, which was quite useful.

We began to make films, sometimes involving a reporter, sometimes not. I gravitated towards certain subjects which could mark festivals or known dates in any year: Easter, the Eisteddfod, Valentine's Day or similar; in other words, I would ensure there would always be a topical peg for a studio link! I went into partnership with Archdruid WJ Gruffydd, a poet with a wicked humour, which provided the commentary for many of these films, later published in book form as *Cerddi'r Llygad* by Gwasg y Dref Wen. I even made a film on Wales' last duel in Newcastle Emlyn, with actors, makeup and real pistols supplied by Barrie.

I know that the powers that be enjoyed these

The Last Duel

mini-epics, but I also know that there were some mutterings about the length of time taken to edit all the effects and music required. (Incidentally, all these films were edited as negatives and switched to positive by telecine.) Nevertheless, I forged ahead. Life is too short for you not to enjoy what you're doing. When we weren't shooting these films deep in the Welsh countryside, I would occasionally work up stories in other places with Welsh connections – especially London. There we did features on subjects as varied as a Welsh chef in the Savoy, Ryan & Ronnie in TV Theatre and a Welsh astronomer. I was now rarely involved in studio direction, having made my niche in film; if anything, I made longer films which filled the whole programme. One of these, I recall, I shot with then reporter R Alun Evans in the famous Gobowen Hospital in North Wales. I suppose all this kind of activity was perfect training for my future place in the features department which I would eventually secure. In fact, I would very often get seconded to other areas of television where new producers required help because of their inexperience with TV direction.

Of these I recall *Cnoi Cil*, a Sunday afternoon show produced by David Bevan and fronted by *Heddiw's* Owen Edwards, which had everything in it, sometimes including the BBC Welsh Orchestra – all live. I have fond memories of programmes presented by poet and broadcaster T Glynne Davies (from Mold) on a range of topics together with *Dilyn Awen* which examined 'inspiration' in many fields. Gareth Price was producer; he would later become Controller and eventually join the Thomson Organisation.

Our first child Elen was born. I did not witness the birth. Bethan's mother, being neurotic about such

With poet and broadcaster T Glynne Davies and critic Frank Price Jones on the shores of Bala Lake

things, insisted that she gave birth in Northlands, an establishment run by nuns who tended to frown on husbands. All went well and we began to feel a proper family in number 7 The Green. We even joined in socially, which was fairly difficult in that very conservative village, and became members of the tennis club. There was a valley train to Cardiff which was useful to both of us since we only had one car – an early Morris 1000 shared with Siân (Bethan's younger sister) who helped pay for it. Later, because of my filming, I bought a battered and bulbous Rover 60. This felt very grand but its performance was unreliable. We got to know several village residents and a BBC designer, Colin Shaw, who lived behind us. He eventually became successful in London.

By now the new Broadcasting House was opened in Llantrisant Road. Built of concrete, glass and river

Elen poses outside our first
house in Radyr

Selwyn the effervescent,
maverick Head of Features

stones from the Taff, it was an impressive sight. I even made a film showing some of its features, with commentary by Alan Protheroe (in his best Hywel Davies voice) which was shown at the opening. It had purpose- built television and radio studios of vast size, together with a concert hall for the orchestra and state-of-the-art BBC club. We, meanwhile, were still in 'General Accident'. This office building slowly emptied as staff began to be transferred to the new Broadcasting House's Features Department, run by the quicksilver, (youngest-ever-TV-producer appointed direct from Oxford) Selwyn Roderick. I summoned up courage and applied...

The inevitable appointment board was assembled and I was called before my 'betters' as the Welsh saying goes. This board was the biggest I had ever faced and included Michael Gill from London (father of AA Gill, the journalist and critic) who ran Features in London and the great Selwyn himself! He also had been a minister's son – poor dab. I must have waffled my way well through this ordeal because on 6 February 1973 I received a memo stating:

'I am pleased to tell you that you have been selected to fill the post of Television Producer, Features and Documentaries, Wales.'

My joy was unbounded. Bethan, Elen and I celebrated that night.

CHAPTER 5

Oh Happy Band

I SOON RECEIVED A HAND-WRITTEN note from Selwyn to
welcome me and say they were looking forward to
my company on my first 'shift' on 1 April that year. My
son Siôn had now been born and with the prospect of
a better salary we moved to a larger but older semi-
detached house in St Michael's Road, Llandaff. Dr
Cann-Jones lived on one side and Dr Keith Jones on
the other, which turned out very handy when childhood
illnesses struck. In a house further down, broadcaster
Vincent Kane and wife Mary lived with their children;
we became firm friends. (When Vince retired they
moved to Cyprus.) Let's face it, at that time Llandaff
and Pontcanna were almost broadcasting ghettos;
now people tend to live further away, even in the Vale.
Some, like George P Owen and his wife Nest still live
in Pencisely Road. We had bought a dog, a golden
retriever called Caradog for Elen; he was a great and
much-loved member of our new home. He was very
intelligent: I would release him at the gate (being lazy)
and he would walk himself to the Insole butcher for a
bone, then come home unsupervised. Ideal!

April arrived and I was shown my office (with
secretary's ante-room) and introduced to other
members of the department. Apart from Selwyn as

Elen and Siôn and our
second house in St.
Michael's Road

head, they were: John Ormond, poet and film maker, who had been running the BBC film unit but now concentrated on his own films, many of which won awards – in particular his portrayal of Polish farmers in Wales; Gethin Stoodley-Thomas, former minesweeper commander, journalist, opera buff and later *Western Mail* film critic; Ivor Rees, former minister, writer of poems and humorous songs, who tended to create portraits of literary figures; and Aled Vaughan, who later left for ITV. Later came Derek Trimby, Rhys Lewis and others as the department expanded. My first secretary or PA was Elisabeth Cameron from Tregaron, inherited from Geraint Stanley, who had left the department to become Head of Programmes. She would shortly follow her old boss to the third floor. I therefore faced the prospect of having to appoint somebody myself! Completely lacking in confidence, I settled for someone I knew from my time in *Heddiw* – Cecily. She was much older than me, but I thought she might give me some gravitas!

Meanwhile my father was coming to terms with his grief and attempting to deal with the death of his daughter in a poem. This turned out to be the crown poem in the Barry National Eisteddfod of 1968.

So there I was, with my own office and a seat in the canteen discussions, an equal among the greats. Soon I got my first programme: *Eagles in Exile* (a documentary about the Polish community in Ceredigion) which would be transmitted on BBC2 on St David's Day. This would be on film – in COLOUR. I had really arrived. It had plenty of characters and colourful festivals, and was well received by the critics. The programme was narrated by my former workmate John Darran, who

My father's crowning in Barry Eisteddfod, 1968

was actually a solicitor who happened to enjoy writing and performing and did the conveyancing on all our houses for a very small fee.

Next came a contribution to a successful BBC 2 documentary called *Look, Stranger* for which I had suggested a story about a Dolgellau solicitor who could only reach his ancient home via the Ffestiniog steam railway, where he had permission to run his own little train on the track. I called the film *The Campbells came by Rail* and we duly commenced shooting on Campbell's Platform in the depths of February.

So dark was it that year that I had to ring Programme Organiser Owen Thomas to tell him we couldn't get a meter reading for colour – what should I do? He was an

The Campbells came by Rail – first Network success

ex-Oxford man and very laid back: 'Sit tight for a day and hope things improve.' Relieved, we all adjourned to the nearest bar. Fortunately things did improve and together with cameraman Robin Rollinson, we captured some magic sequences. I would do more epics with Robin during my BBC career. Editing the film in London's Television Centre, my editor and I became aware that the film rushes had been disturbed overnight. We discovered that the series editor, Jennifer Jeremy, had been taking it to show her boss to gauge his opinion. We didn't need to worry and had it had the potential for expansion, it could have spawned a series, as did *Blaster Bates* and another film about a steeplejack. Nancy Banks-Smith rhapsodised about the film in the London papers and I began to gain confidence.

Another duty we had in Features was covering national events like the National Eisteddfod, the Llangollen Eisteddfod and the Royal Welsh. I co-produced these with Selwyn and worked with several well-known names: Richard Baker, Cy Grant, John Humphrys and Sue Lawley among others; and thoroughly enjoyed the experience and their company in spite of my hay fever which still flared up in the summer months. Most of these programmes were in English for the London network but I also was in charge of Welsh output which ultimately led me to be responsible for the total BBC National Eisteddfod TV coverage.

Back at home (whenever I could get there) I was surprisingly recognised by the two children, whilst Bethan taught French at the Bishop of Llandaff School. In Rhondda my parents were getting older; my father was on the verge of retirement and my mother (still in active mourning) was ailing. It was obvious that something had to be done for them. We began to search for a new home, somewhere that could accommodate all of us. At that time I also befriended a colleague, John Stuart Roberts, who was a producer in Religious Programmes and lived in the same road in Llandaff. He was a frequent visitor and, together with his wife Verina and children, we would go on foreign trips together, either to France or Italy. Travelling by car, in tandem, we had great times together and the children got on well.

By now our third child Gwenllian had been born, a bouncing, curly-haired girl, doted on by the two older children. As luck would have it (and luck is very important in this life) we discovered a large house, Littlegate, an 'Edwardian gentleman's detached residence' sitting in its own grounds at the junction of Llandaff Road and Fairwater Road. It was rather run-down and surprisingly owned by an ear, nose and throat specialist whose wife was from Aberaeron and knew my father well. I took my parents to see it and we clinched the deal. I think it cost £38,000, which we managed to scrape together by including the sale (for £10,000) of a tiny property in Oxford Street, Aberaeron which I managed to sell to a BBC colleague. The only thing we didn't like was the name and decided to change it to Llys Aeron as soon as possible. I bought some slate nameplates in a stall at the Eisteddfod that year in readiness for the move. This would become our home for the rest of my BBC career. Fortuitously, Bethan was appointed Head of French in the nearby Welsh-language comprehensive, Ysgol Glantaf. My son

Elen, Siôn and Gwenllian

Llys Aeron,
now demolished

Siôn started there the same year whilst Elen continued to journey to Ysgol Llanhari near Pontyclun and Gwenllian still attended Ysgol Bryntaf in the Parade in the city.

The new house, compared with our other homes, was big and rambling, with a panelled entrance hall leading to an elegant grand staircase. It even had a servants' back staircase and scullery with slate cold store. What was more, it had six potential bedrooms to accommodate the family. There was a very large lounge, dining room and sitting room which would serve as a base for my parents, and could therefore solve all our problems. The children loved it. What it didn't have were mod cons and it was obvious we needed to spend on improvements, e.g. a new kitchen, bathroom and shower room, as well as expenditure on the outside and grounds. You may notice that I hadn't written any poetry during this period, for example celebrating the children's births. This is probably a function of just how busy in creative terms my work had become. By the time my grandchildren arrived, things changed and I had time on my hands. I was always to celebrate their births with a poem.

Meanwhile I was always busy with some programme or other. We had an OB series called *Penigamp*, which I co-produced with Teleri Bevan in what seemed like every village hall in Wales. I even directed the XIth Welsh Games with presenter Ron Pickering! But the time had come for something more 'dramatic'. During a conversation with Geraint Stanley (who was now Head of Programmes) I offered one idea about which he immediately enthused. Thinking about my Aberaeron grandmother, I said, 'Why don't we try to recreate some of the fervour of the Revival – 1904 and all that – in dramatic form?' He blinked and thought, 'Do you think you could?' Within a few minutes, I had the brief to investigate the potential and perhaps to find a screenwriter. I bumped into Teleri Bevan in the corridor, who said, 'Why don't you try Paul Ferris from Swansea? He's very good at writing biogs on interesting people.' So it was that *The Revivalist* was born.

Sketty-born Paul Ferris, as it turned out, lived in Putney and was busy writing articles for the London papers, but would see me. I went hot foot to London. 'We should base it on a Swansea newspaper editor's perspective,' he said, loving the idea of doing a portrait of his home area – Loughor especially. Paul was best known for his probing biographies rather than his drama, but his enthusiasm for drama-documentaries was infectious and he had the journalist's scepticism for this particular subject which mirrored my own. He also had the maturity and confidence to boost my morale, which was beginning to flag at the prospect of actually portraying the fervour of a revival. So we were off. It was agreed that it could all be done on film and that BBC2 would pick up the tab. The film would concentrate on the last six months of Evan Roberts' short ministry. Critic Clive James was eventually to call it 'enthralling', but we had a long way to go before then...

I established a habit here which I continued during future drama productions: I never discussed projects with writers in the office (e.g. Ferris, Meic Povey and Harri Webb) but preferred day-long script sessions at home with them in Llys Aeron. There would thrash out treatments and ideas, ensuring that there were no surprises or problems with final scripts when delivered.

First came the problem of recreating the hysterical meetings and the singing; this would be solved with the help of Towyn Jones (no mean storyteller himself), minister of Heol Awst Chapel, Carmarthen, who would arrange the congregations. These would be supplemented by a sprinkling professional actors. Next the casting. North Wales-born actor Gareth Thomas (of *Stocker's Copper* and *Blake's 7* fame) looked very much like Evan Roberts and certainly had the ability. The veteran editor and his sister would be played by John Phillips and Beryl Williams; Evan's mother, brother and

Gareth Thomas as Evan Roberts, *The Revivalist*

sister by Rachel Thomas, Ian Saynor and Lesley Dunlop, with supporting roles played by the best we could book for the duration of the shoot. The cameraman would be Robin Rollinson (again), the designer Pauline Harrison and the editor Bill Mainman. Location work started in Marshfield outside Cardiff (standing in for Loughor) and eventually ended in Gwaelod y Garth and Carmarthen where the revival was staged. I was assisted by Myrfyn Owen (now unfortunately deceased) who was very helpful in working up the hysteria in the various chapels.

The film, transmitted on Good Friday 1976 on BBC2 was declared 'Pick of the Day' by all the London critics and, even better for me, 'a success' by management. In a way, this was the turning point in my career, since it meant I now had some credibility with London controllers which would stand me in good stead for the next few years. It would also give me clout regionally and afford me the artistic independence I craved and a higher profile with colleagues.

However successful a project, it belongs to the past and the *next* project becomes a priority. This was not long in coming. In the meantime I would experience a little *divertissement*, because being in Features demanded an ability to adapt instantly to new challenges. In this case it was the Sixth International World Harp Contest to be held in September in Israel! Ann Griffiths, renowned Welsh harpist, was taking one of her students, 17-year-old Caryl Thomas from Carmarthen, to compete in this prestigious event in Jerusalem. The Six-Day War had only recently finished, so I approached the trip with some trepidation.

I met Ann who had been to Israel and even knew key

words in the language (I stuck to 'Shalom'). She was a dynamic tutor in Cardiff's College of Music and Drama and was a very determined lady. The only limitation she would admit to, would be a recurring backache from humping a concert harp for so many years. We sat down together in her fine house in Gilwern and I drafted some ideas which might be suitable. There was no recce – we would shoot on the hoof. Now, surprisingly, I hadn't flown any distance before this and the prospect of having to get cans of colour film stock through customs on my own was worrying. Our crew would already be there. They were from the Israel Broadcasting Authority (IBA) and normally shot in monochrome from the hip!

September arrived and Bethan ran me to Heathrow to catch the EL-AL jumbo to Tel Aviv. As luck would have it, the Israeli Embassy had ensured my passage through the VIP suite and I sailed through the normally rigorous checks. I said farewell to Bethan and 'passed through to the other side'. There in the boarding lounge were a smiling Ann and Caryl together with harpist Val Aldrich-Smith who came as support. Accompanied by my PA Cecily, we travelled in some style to Ben Gurion airport and landed to the sound of joyful Israeli songs being sung by relieved passengers returning home. It was night. Coming out of the concourse was like stepping into an oven. We were met by cameraman Shraga and David Michaeli (IBA liaison man) and transported to the Hotel Moriah in the centre of modern Jerusalem where we collapsed into our respective beds. The following morning I opened the curtains and could hardly believe the view. In front of me was a complete panorama of the old city walls, its towers and minarets, all bathed in

Three harpists in Galilee: Caryl, Ann and Val

an incredibly dazzling white light. All of Jerusalem, by decree, was built in the region's traditional sandstone. I was gobsmacked.

By ten o'clock we had a lift with Shraga to the IBA HQ; there it was unnerving to notice the level of security and the lounging military commissionaires with Uzi machine-guns within easy reach. We sat down in an office to discuss my projected schedule. The first idea to be rejected was any filming outdoors between noon and 3.30pm. The sun would be too high and everybody's eyes would look like 'piss-holes in the snow – and it would be too hot anyway'. Everything else was more or less possible.

Shraga was an interesting character who wore a permanent 'Dai cap' and had a glass eye. He had foolishly picked up a live grenade as a child, leading to the loss of an eye and some fingers. He was, nevertheless, senior cameraman at IBA. Originally from Haifa, he had seen a great deal of action, knew everybody and was

Shraga Merchav, typically filming hand-held

friendly with many Arabs, even living in an interesting octagonal house in the Arab quarter. We became great friends and he later stayed with us in Llys Aeron, his brother-in-law being one-time Israeli ambassador to London. We eventually drafted a schedule that would encompass the competition in the Jerusalem Theatre and allow us to explore Israel between times.

Thus started a wonderful fortnight that I shall never forget. For a Rhondda boy to visit all these places, with what seemed Welsh biblical names, was unforgettable. Even Shraga was surprised that when I pronounced Hebrew names as if they were Welsh, the pronunciation was correct. I had always known that the Welsh were the 'lost tribe of Israel'! I fell in love with Israel, which may have been because it never rained. In fact, they took off car wipers between April and November in case they were stolen. As it turned out, we managed

to travel from the Lebanon border (the Golan Heights) and Galilee in the north, to the Negev, where I bathed in the Dead Sea, in the south. Of course, Israel is only about the length of Wales and all this was easily accomplished. We even found time to cover the harp competition!

The closing night of the competition finally arrived, a gala evening where Caryl, the youngest-ever competitor, picked up a prize. Cecily and I said our goodbyes and, after getting our precious film stamped by Israeli security in Jerusalem, we headed home from Tel Aviv. The film was eventually transmitted by BBC2, entitled *Their Harps of Gold*, a reference to a quote by King David.

My goodness, what could be next? That experience would take some beating. My previous liaison with Paul Ferris brought me swiftly to the next film. Paul had always been Dylan Thomas' biographer and was keen that we attempt to tackle his life story. Preliminary talks with BBC2 Controller Aubrey Singer led to an OK for development. I was familiar with Dylan's work

Even I was given a limited edition Chagall medal – for directing!

having read his collected poems in my early teens. My father had, of course, won the Eisteddfod crown for his valedictory poem on Dylan. Not that we were particularly enamoured with Dylan's lifestyle, but the rhythms and cadences of his poems, although crafted in English, had a mood and resonance which was very Welsh. I can even now see his influences in some of the verses that I produced, masquerading as poetry!

Paul and I were very aware from the outset that Dylan's widow Caitlin (then living in Italy) would have nothing to do with such a film so we had to exclude any portrayal of her which would lead to litigation. So we decided to limit her involvement to one moment (in long shot!) and concentrate on the last year of Dylan's life (with flashbacks) when he was being feted in the USA and had an affair with Liz Reitell. This would probably be my biggest project so far; this being so, Paul was instantly commissioned to write the script and I began the long pre-production process. It would be on film, with scenes shot here and in the Eastern USA. Selwyn had used a Cardiff-born researcher, Ann Cowie, on one of his many safaris there and she agreed to meet me. A recce schedule was hastily drawn up which would include New York, Baltimore and Washington, and I started selecting a crew.

Any added clout I had from *The Revivalist* was useful, because I was practically able to pick my own crew. Robin would be on camera, Bill Mainman would be editor, Marina Monios makeup, and Pearl Sedgefield from Rhondda would be costume designer. Unusually for a drama production, there would be two set designers: Peter Phillips (who would be responsible for the American mood) and Pauline Harrison (who had been on *The Revivalist* building the sets and overlooking the Welsh shooting). Also unusual was that I would have several assistants, in particular Gwyn Hughes Jones and Mike Wright (who was on attachment from Design and was with me in Trinity). Myrfyn would also be there to assist me. There were also two PAs: my own, Cecily, and Myra Jervis (a Glaswegian who had married a Welsh engineer). There were many others of course. The redoubtable, quicksilver Ken Hawkins would monitor expenditure back in the Beeb.

I started some preliminary casting. We secured the services of many fine players: Gayle Hunnicutt, a beautiful Texan star to play Liz, Dylan's mistress; Clifford Evans to play Dylan's father; Rhoda Lewis, his mother. American actors resident in London would play American parts: Ed Bishop, Toby Robins, Phil Brown, Christopher Muncke, Kate Harper and Valerie Colgan; Welsh actors like William Thomas and Rachel Thomas had big roles.

However, I still hadn't found my Dylan. Time was

pressing and Paul's script was nearing completion. There was also the matter of the USA recce. I had to go, accompanied by designer Peter Phillips; Robin was to join us later from Rome where he was filming. As we were preparing a recce schedule, I received a call from Mervyn Williams (then Head of Music). Since I was going to the USA could I fit in a film for him? No, nothing to do with Dylan; he wanted to cover the Polyphonic Choir's tour of California and could I help? This, as you might say, put 'another layer on the cake'. Mad though I must have been and a sucker to boot, I agreed. This meant more arranging and another schedule to devise for yet another film crew! If I had been the age I am now, I probably would have slit my throat.

Peter Phillips and I managed to get to JFK via Heathrow and arrived at the Algonquin Hotel at about 2am where we watched in amazement the plethora of TV channels in our bedroom. The next morning we caught up with Ann Cowie who had travelled up from her home in Baltimore to meet us. We recceed all the sites: the Algonquin (literary haunt), the bar of the White Horse Tavern (Dylan's favourite watering hole) and the Chelsea Hotel (where he eventually died). The recces went well and after two days we left for Baltimore where we needed to set up halls in the Johns Hopkins University and facilities which involved period trains – courtesy of the Baltimore & Ohio Railroad Museum. It was in our base at Ann's grand house in Longwood Drive near the university (her husband David was a psychiatrist at the university hospital) that I first tasted the American lifestyle and approach to problems. I think the keynote is 'can-do'. Had I been on recce in

Researcher Ann Cowie, cameraman Robin Rollinson and designer Peter Phillips recce Delaware

the UK, the response was usually: 'Oh, that's tricky,' or, 'It might take some time to arrange.' In Baltimore *all* was possible. 'You need a period train – where would you like us to put it?' 'You wanna have students? How many and when?' This experience rubbed off, giving me a positive approach to problem-solving for many years after.

I was given full use of the large Schriver Hall on the campus and as many students as would be required for filming, as I remember, at no charge. A large period American engine and carriages would be in a siding on Baltimore station! Ann would organise things so that the students would be in '50s clothes. This was all looking easy and with my confidence high, I boarded a

121

Producer visits the Chelsea Hotel, Dylan's last base in New York

Peter, Robin, and assistant cameramen Gerald Cobbe and Paul Reed recce the roof of the Chelsea Hotel

flight from Washington via Dallas to LA International airport for my next recce. I think I was the only passenger. I well remember the pilot speaking on the tannoy the entire time: 'On your right, there's me mom, on her lonesome in dear old Albuquerque, New Mexico; sure wish we could stop over...'

Six hours after leaving Washington, I landed in LA to be met by an exiled Welshman working there. Dr Terry James, a somewhat eccentric conductor and composer, had been there for some years, composing music for film. Accompanied by his chauffeur and wearing a cardigan and bowler, he met me at LA's Union Station. He greeted me in Welsh and his silent companion drove

Prospective presidential candidate barred from the Oval Office

Dr Terry James and
friend welcome
me outside Union
Station, Los Angeles

us in the limo to Hollywood's Sunset Boulevard. There we had tea in Terry's 'pad', an apartment consisting of a grand piano, a manuscript-strewn desk, kitchen and large bed. It might have been September, but it was damn hot! He had found me a motel next door which would suffice for a few days. This had a bed which, if you inserted a dime, would vibrate...

Dr Terry was bonhomie personified and very kind. For the next two days he drove me around Hollywood, regaling me with stories of his exploits with the stars and showing me the delights of Bel-Air and Santa Monica Beach. He looked forward to meeting friends he knew in the Polyphonic Choir when they arrived.

Exhausted by the welcome and heat, I was glad to board the Coastal Starlight Express for San Francisco for the next leg of this amazing journey. There I was scheduled to meet BBC Wales cameraman Russ Walker and Mansel Davies his sound recordist in a grand hotel on Market Street in the Bay. Russ, a Scot, was a stalwart of the BBC camera unit who had spent most of his career in Wales. He was also very strong and could 'shoot from the hip' when required. We got on well. He had hired an enormous American estate car to use as our transport and filming platform; in this we set out for Fort Bragg on the northern coast of California where we would rendezvous with the choir who were already in Oregon. Arriving in the teeth of a sudden Pacific storm which lashed the coast, we eventually made contact with the choir, including Richard Elfyn (the conductor) and his wife, Ieuan Lewis (who was himself a BBC director) Gareth Bowen (a BBC news editor, father of reporter Jeremy Bowen) and many others, a reduced version of the normal choir. I won't bore you with detail, but there

Cactus doesn't offer much shade (the cactus is on the right)

Sweltering, near Palm Springs, we await the passage of the Choir bus

followed days of tracking their bus, their concerts and their thoughts as they toured the 'Golden State'. At one point I had to drive the ghastly estate wagon (Ieuan Lewis deputising on the bus as director) and made the 402 miles down Interstate 5 to LA. How I kept awake I shall never know. The road ran straight as an arrow through what seemed like desert. We all met up (plus undamaged estate wagon) in the Roosevelt Hotel on Hollywood Boulevard opposite the famous Chinese Theatre. There we managed a break by the pool and, surprisingly, whipped up some energy to film vox pops! After my driving experience, I decided to call the film *Intermezzo on Interstate 5*. Back in the brilliant sunshine, we ploughed on (after a Hollywood concert) to the south of this amazing state while the weather got hotter.

We got as far as the Mexican border and the town of Tijuana where the Interstate 5 petered out into a dirt track. There, the hall had cockroaches in the audience. Then back north along the coast via San Diego (and would you believe 'Cardiff-on-Sea'), Santa Barbara, Carmel and Monterey (delightful) and eventually 'Frisco with its incredible Golden Gate and Bay. We did closing interviews on a boat trip around Alcatraz Island, said our goodbyes, and I headed for Oakland Airport and boarded a Laker Skytrain (now defunct) to face the 13-hour flight home. It had all been a mind-blowing experience and I had been amazed at the warmth not only of the American people but also of the ex-pats who came in droves to the concerts and spoke to camera about their *hiraeth* for home.

One young student, doubtless brought up on a diet of pop and rock, exclaimed: 'I think, I... uh know, I...

Outside Ann Cowie's house in Baltimore

Family group outside The Capitol

uh ain't never been exposed to anything like this...' It would be some years before I returned (with wife and three children) to Baltimore – on holiday that time.

On my return home there was no time for a holiday. The schedule at the Welsh end was firming up and most of the cast settled. Filming dates were looming, but where was my Dylan? I happened to see the *Mayor of Casterbridge* on TV, starring one Ronald Lacey. Thinking we might have found a Dylan look-alike, I leapt to *Spotlight* (the casting bible) and looked him up. Yes, he certainly looked the part. He already had a name as a character actor. I rang his agent; would he come to Cardiff to audition? Yes he would.

In the interim, I showed his photo to Marina and asked her opinion. Yes, she said, but he would probably need at least two wigs since he would also have to play Dylan in his twenties. So one day, I waited in anticipation at Llys Aeron expecting his knock on the front door. Eventually, I heard a distant knock at the back kitchen door! It was Ronald, or 'Ronnie', as we thereafter called him. Once in the lounge, I could instantly see that as the older Dylan he would have no problem; the younger could surely be solved by Marina. The biggest shock I had was his voice. He spoke in a high cockney accent with none of the timbre and resonance associated with Dylan. Dylan's voice *had* to be recreated, otherwise the film would have no credibility. Half an hour later, my colleague Myrfyn Owen called (to give a second opinion as it were) and eventually we wound up the interview and Ronnie returned home, to Pontypool, as it emerged, where he had a holiday cottage.

Once he'd gone, Myrfyn voiced his opinion. He thought Ronnie was more than capable of surmounting

A final chance to see the amazing twin towers of The World Trade Centre – this was 1979

any problems and was a superb character actor. Before leaving, Ronnie had asked to be sent tapes of Dylan and I compiled a tape of the dialogue personally since I could do a passable imitation of his voice – well, at least I thought it was passable! Within a week, Ronnie had returned my tape and included one of his version of Dylan. Listening to this my relief was tangible. We had found our Dylan! I didn't know then that, having a slightly reddish tinge in the hair department, Ronnie had a quick temper and also 'carried a bag', having had an abdominal op in his late teens. All this would emerge later. We were on our way…

CHAPTER 6

The Life and Death
of a Poet

I HAVE ALWAYS BELIEVED IN the importance of the filming schedule. A well-devised plan of action can be the key to efficiency, cost saving, best use of the actors and can help control the ultimate cost of the film. To me, making the schedule is not a chore but an integral part of the process – a mixture of art and science! My schoolboy interest in chess stood me in good stead. Like chess, any move in the schedule has multiple ramifications. How you load it can affect the performance of not only actors, but the rest of the crew. On average, we would shoot seven scenes a day, but in order to maximise the time, allow for makeup and costume changes, lighting and track-laying, the planning needed detailed consideration. Often, actors appreciate a heavier load in the morning and a lighter schedule in the afternoon, since their energy levels can dip dramatically at around three o'clock. How much load one gives in the day can also affect any subsequent night shoot. Actors' availability is obviously crucial. Continuity can also be a major problem. For example, there was a sequence in *Dylan* which intercut two sets: one in the Dolman Theatre, Newport and the other

3,000 miles and some weeks later in the USA. This involved the following:

1   Dolman stage wings – Dylan arrives for lecture and is ill
2   USA – Student audience applaud with anticipation
3   Dolman wings – Dylan enters stage
4   USA – Dylan continues entrance
5   Dolman lecterns – Dylan positions himself for poetry reading
6   USA – Wide-angle stage from audience
7   Dolman stage – Close-ups Dylan readings, intercut with
8   USA – audience rapture.

This kind of sequence demands not only continuity from the continuity girl, the lighting crew, makeup and wardrobe, but also continuity of performance from the actor, supervised by the director. Although there are now computer programmes available offering scheduling short cuts (e.g. *Movie Magic*), I, for one, am not convinced that they are a substitute for considered or intelligent thought. I'm pleased to see that my younger daughter Gwenllian, also in the business, favours the old approach: shunting pieces of paper around!

So it was, in the late autumn of '77 that we shot our first sequence: the younger Dylan doing a poetry reading in a sound studio (mocked up on a studio set) with his producer and secretary listening in a cubicle. Marina's biggest task was probably that of making Ronnie look at least 10 years younger, coupled with a transformation for the next scene (in a rocking mock-up of an old railway carriage) to a much older Dylan. A difficult day for us all, especially Ronnie, who had to

Dylan's film crew pose outside his work shed in Laugharne

quickly establish the character and stick with it! But it went well and we pressed on with added confidence.

To cut a long story short, we continued filming for several hectic weeks in Wales. Locations were as varied as Cardiff's Royal Hotel, Laugharne's Boat House and Dylan's work hut (I believe our set and dressing is still there), West Wales churchyards and a duplication of Dylan's room in the Chelsea Hotel, New York (complete with skyscraper view) built in an old hospital in Llandaff. We had tremendous co-operation from the villagers in Laugharne as we recreated a radio broadcast of *Our Town* in the village hall, portraying the arrival of a telegram informing them of Dylan's premature death.

BROWN'S HOTEL RE-VISITED

In cosy closet
Brown
The froth-encircled
Fists still clutch
Anew the
Amber oil that
Lubricates the
Laughter,
Song and
Echoed mirth of
Yesteryear
In parsimonious streets
By parish pump, the prim
Pariah's swoop and
Gobble up a myriad
Titbit truths and
Lies, as they then
Wagtailed,
Bustled
Flee to
Spinstered sofas, there,
To swallow and
Regurgitate their
Tawdry tales of
Tom or Dick or
Harry,
That loyal
But
Unholy Trinity;

Stigmatas
Given free,
On throat,
On thigh, or
Knee.

(RL *Poems 1977)*

I particularly enjoyed recreating New York's Grand Central station in Cardiff's Temple of Peace. We were followed by the press at every turn. They were drawn by Gayle Hunnicutt's presence, although anything to do with Dylan has perennial interest. When you consider that Ronnie neither smoked nor drank, he settled well into the role. He was not over-thrilled by the media attention given to Gayle, but I never had any problems with him; you would never believe that he had carried a colostomy bag since his adolescence.

Whilst we in Wales carried on filming into the winter, with its frost and gaunt, leaf-less trees (great for mood), Ann Cowie was setting up USA locations, squaring things up with the New York Mayor's office and securing student audiences. As February 1978 approached, some twenty of the crew prepared to wrap shooting in Wales and de-camp to the States. I was particularly worried about the militant Truckers Union; they had a powerful grip on the American film industry and we couldn't afford to cross them in any way. I decided that, if anybody asked, we were doing a documentary on Dylan (avoiding the term 'drama') and that we would co-opt two members of the said union to assist with lighting. These reservations aside, we flew off to the New World. A violent winter storm

Gayle Hunnicutt as Liz Reitell, Dylan's 'friend' in New York

greeted our arrival in JFK (I think they subsequently closed the runway), then we struggled to Newark for a connecting flight to Washington, surrounded by senators and typewriters.

Our first shoot was scheduled in Baltimore station, where we found our period diesel train and three carriages. I have never been so cold. American wind comes from the Arctic. My brain froze. Ronnie's 'Dylan cigarette' stuck to his lips and he wasn't at all well. Nevertheless, we soldiered on and shot the opening sequence for the film: a modern diesel shunting the period diesel back and fore on cue, as Dylan said farewell to two American lecturers. It speaks volumes for Ronnie's professionalism that he managed to keep going, let alone stay in character...

Our next challenge would be to whip up student reaction to Dylan as we recreated several different readings in Johns Hopkins University campus halls. I needn't have worried. The students turned up in their hundreds, all in costume, all reacting as if Dylan himself was present! When the moment for filming arrived, I was approached by Gwyn Hughes Jones and Mike Wright, both ashen-faced and whispering: 'It's Ronnie – he's staying down in the dressing room – he won't come on!' It needed only one look at their faces for me to know that this was a major crisis. I rushed down to the dressing room. There in full Dylan costume and wig stood Ronnie, incandescent and trembling with rage! Had he cracked? Would I be left with six hundred students baying for my blood? No, he hadn't cracked, he was just having an actor's attack of pique (with all the stops out) having heard Myrfyn on the tannoy doing an audience warm-up and telling Dylan-type jokes. In any event, Ronnie didn't think he was being paid enough. I spent ten minutes calming him down, promising anything, even a pay rise, saying how wonderful his performance was (here I was telling the truth) and reluctantly he calmed down and agreed to appear.

As he entered the stage, you could have sworn that the Messiah had arrived! He gave a superb performance, the students loved it and you could have thought that the events in the dressing room had never happened. In reality, the pressures on Ronnie were immense and his body was getting very tired, hence the tantrums. Putting in a fine performance, week in week out, had taken its toll. After finishing our shoot he was off to Hollywood, then South Africa to play a reporter in the

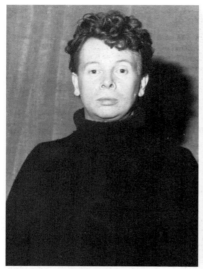

The expertise of Marina Monios, makeup artist, transformed Ronnie from the young Dylan, to his wild days in London, and finally to his last days in the White Horse Tavern in New York

Ronnie performs at the lectern in front of an American student audience

We remained good
friends throughout
the filming period

film *Zulu Dawn* and we still had New York to face.

After a farewell dance in the University, where we presented prizes for the best-dressed-in-period-costume to students, we de-camped for the Big Apple. Some went by Amtrak, others by car. The majority went in the bus, driven gallantly by Mike Wright. Thankfully, it was warmer there and the city throbbed with air conditioning. We had quite few sequences here including:

1 Chelsea Hotel and staircase (to be intercut with scenes already shot in Llandaff)
2 Algonquin Hotel interior
3 A scene with Gayle in Madison Square
4 The first *Under Milk Wood* reading on stage at the Kaufman Auditorium
5 Exteriors of the White Horse Tavern in Greenwich Village
6 A night scene with Gayle on Brooklyn Heights.

The latter was set on a street which overlooked the whole illuminated panorama of New York (fortunately excluding the Twin Towers which weren't there in Dylan's day) and was difficult to light. I was amazed at how knowledgeable the two cops sent to guard us were; they quoted 'Fern Hill' and other Dylan poems. I doubt we would have heard anything similar from UK bobbies in similar circumstances. Dylan was still very big in New York and everyone seemed to know something about him. In fact, filming in New York was less hassle than if we had been in London; we were not harassed by the Truckers Union and overall the welcome was warm and supportive – typically American. I had been particularly concerned about the daylight scene in Madison Square with its famous period flat-iron skyscraper, but even there (although I had released non-essential staff in order to maintain a low profile) we had no problems. The final scene of Dylan meeting Liz Reitell and doing his first *Under Milk Wood* reading at New York's Poetry Centre passed without incident. I can still hear Ronnie's evocative interpretation of the closing lines...

So that was it. A few drinks and hurried goodbyes after the 'wrap' was called and we all went our separate ways: Ronnie to Hollywood, Gayle and husband Simon Jenkins continuing their USA break, while others stayed on with wives or boyfriends who had joined them. I returned hotfoot to Cardiff. There, Bethan had entrusted the children to her mother and arranged that we go (with Siân and husband David) by car to Paris for a few days' break! After those hothouse months of filming and the air conditioning in the States, I nearly died as Paris suffered its coldest Easter for years. Bethan always reminds me that I found a patch of sunlight outside Napoleon's Tomb and collapsed, saying: 'I'm not moving from here!' It goes without saying that I was, by then, like a zombie, which is normal after a long shoot. We returned to Cardiff where I would spend several months alone with editor Bill Mainman trying to get our rushes into some semblance of order whilst I recovered slowly.

The film was scheduled for transmission on BBC2 in early November 1978, so we laboured to produce a print which could be shown at London's BAFTA HQ in October. There we knew we could expect all the main reviewers and critics to assemble (knives sharpened) to assess the success or failure of our project. Such was the attraction of the Dylan label that we had a full house. Luminaries such as Clive James, Sean Day-Lewis, Nancy Banks-Smith, Alexander Walker and Barry Took filled the front seats. Ronnie sat in the back with his wife and daughter Rebecca Lacey. We needn't have worried. Their reviews say it all and we could face transmission with confidence. Ronnie, genuinely moved, could only whisper: 'Thanks Dic... mate.'

My favourite comments came from Douglas Cleverdon (Dylan's original radio producer) in the *Radio Times*. He said, 'I was much relieved when *Dylan* turned out to be an admirable, indeed, an exemplary programme of its kind. Even in close-up, Lacy looked more like Dylan than any human being could be reasonably expected to look. BBC Wales may well regard *Dylan* as a heron's feather in its cap.'

However, in spite of the critical acclaim and plaudits and the huge mailbag of congratulatory letters received, Ronnie was not to receive a deserved BAFTA award for his efforts. BAFTA was very English-orientated then (as now) and more well-known names were in the frame that year. The benefits of a star name! Undeterred, I committed the same 'crime' on my next film project *Nye* (also written by Paul Ferris) on the life of Aneurin Bevan. Here, I cast John Hartley, an established character actor from Yorkshire, in the title role. For me, the suspension of disbelief was crucial in drama documentaries and you needed someone who could be credible – even to those who knew the principal character. I always felt that casting 'stars' was unproductive. Cary Grant, for example, was always Cary Grant irrespective of the character he was meant to be playing. I exclude certain players from this slur; e.g. Anthony Hopkins, who at least goes to some lengths to achieve verisimilitude, as seen in his portrayal of Nixon. One has also to avoid the mimic or impressionist's trick of giving a superficial view of the character. It is honesty that one looks for, together with an ability to sustain a true representation over a long period of filming. All these characteristics I found in John Hartley, as well as an incredible likeness to the main character. Not unsurprisingly, he had often been called 'Nye' by his parents. And so it was that we soldiered on to the next epic which would be for Alan Hart, Controller of BBC1!

I must also declare here my appreciation of the support I received at this time from Geraint as Head of Programmes, together with my departmental head Selwyn, whose effervescent enthusiasm was constant. Although they sometimes looked quizzically at me as if I were some renegade pupil who deserved a thrashing, they were always ready with support and kindly advice. Yet neither actively interfered and I continued to feel that I was creatively independent.

I do not intend to go into detail about this or any subsequent film lest this becomes tedious. The filming proceeded well as we covered locations as various as Brighton, Tredegar, Nye's actual farm in the home counties and complicated studio recreations (with electronic inlays) of the House of Commons. Alan Hart was eventually to say (after a viewing): 'This will go well in our nine o'clock slot.' Prime time and *fame* at last for yours truly!

We faced the same problem in *Nye* as we encountered in *Dylan.* Some key relatives were still alive; in particular, Nye's wife Jenny Lee and a sister. Although

Nye and his mother, played by Rachel Thomas

Nye attracted plenty of newspaper coverage in Brighton and in the South Wales valleys

Oscar Quitak (as Hugh Gaitskell), John Hartley, and Reginlad Marsh (as Richard Crossman)

144

Paul had spoken at length to both ladies during his research, it was fairly obvious from their responses that they would take a dim view of any dramatic portrayal of Nye. So, yet again, we attempted to tell the story with as limited reference to relatives as was possible or indeed credible. *Nye* was well received by the critics, but not embraced by his sister or wife. In general, and understandably, relatives do not respond well to portrayals of their loved ones on film, no matter how accurate or well-intentioned the representation.

It was about this time that my father and mother came to live with us in Llys Aeron. My father had now retired from the ministry and we had plenty of room. We also made sure that August was fairly free for us to continue our habit of going to France. Bethan was by now Head of French at Ysgol Glantaf and needed to go often; I followed and caught the bug. We eventually bought a static caravan near Grasse, then a village house in Charente-Maritime surrounded by sunflowers which we refurbished slowly. Charente is the second sunniest place in France but is cold in winter. It was very much a summer pad which required constant attention to battle the damp. Nevertheless, we had good times there and cycled a lot or bathed in the salt-water pool nearby. In the end, as the children got older and were in work, it was decided that it was too inaccessible. We then moved everything to a flat in Nice – a cosy bolthole which we still maintain, and to which our children can fly in less than two hours.

Latching on to what was now my niche in network drama-documentary, I embarked on two more films with writer Paul Ferris (who had since moved to a period house in mid Wales). The first was *The Extremist* starring

Our first home in France – a static caravan near Cannes

Our second – a village house in Charrente-Maritime

Our third – a top floor flat in Nice

Senior citizens (with Welsh flag) enjoying the sunny terrace above Rue Rossini

146

Dyfed Thomas. This was a portrayal of John Jenkins, who led the campaign against the investiture of the Prince of Wales in 1969 by Mudiad Amddiffyn Cymru (Movement for the Defence of Wales). The film co-starred Philip Madoc, Aubrey Richards and Clifford Evans, and gave Dyfed a great opportunity to give a chilling portrayal of a largely lone operator and his attempt to rock the establishment. Shot on location in Caernarfon and various reservoirs in North Wales, it also intercut with recordings of the actual investiture. Since I had attended that event, a certain verisimilitude was assured.

In order to ensure an accurate portrait, I arranged for John Jenkins to come to see me at home, which he eventually agreed to do. I found the quiet resolve he still exhibited, in spite of his having served a jail sentence and now being a social worker, quite chilling. But he agreed that we could go ahead and that he would meet Dyfed for a chat. However, he did say that he was convinced that Special Branch still had him under surveillance, which made me wonder if there was a shadowy figure outside in Fairwater Road watching this particular meeting. Afterwards, I reflected on the unsettling nature of this first encounter with an 'extremist'. On the one hand, I admired his continued steely resolve and the frustrated nationalism which had initiated his actions, but on the other hand we couldn't be seen to condone his methods. Bombs, as we all know in these terrorist-ridden days, have a habit of injuring innocent bystanders or explode wide of their target. Because of this, we ensured that the Clifford Evans' mentor character would lecture Jenkins, warning him of the dangers of violent action during several scenes in the film.

Veteran actor Clifford Evans playing opposite Dyfed Thomas in *The Extremist*

I think that although the film was considered a success, there were voices raised (amongst the royalists) in meetings which questioned the portrayal of such an extremist...

I covered less controversial ground with my next film, written by up-and-coming writer Meic Povey. *Babylon Bypassed* was pure drama and examined the tensions between two young lovers from different social backgrounds in the Merthyr Valley, attempting to succeed not only in love but also in life. This had cameos from Bob Blythe, Maggie John, Aubrey Richards and Ray Smith, whose last film this was. In contrast to this tragic tale I moved into comedy with Ryan Davies in *How Green was My Father* (BBC2), a *tour de force* performance by Ryan in which he plays practically all the characters, including the main role of a Yank searching for his roots in Rhondda. My wife always remembers gales of laughter in the garden of Llys Aeron as writer Harri Webb, Ryan and myself invented plot lines and dialogue.

This was a difficult film to shoot because of the time required for makeup and wardrobe changes, and the fact that Ryan was playing opposite himself in practically every sequence. But we managed to produce a winner which is a permanent record of the now-late Ryan's multiple talents. The cameraman was Russ Walker; thank God for his Scottish strength and patience!

Ryan as the archtypal Yank searching for his Welsh roots, observed by Russ Walker and the director

Ryan benefits from my experience of having suffered at the hands of irate schoolmasters

During this period I moved out of Broadcasting House to some offices in Gabalfa estate which were occupied by several departments including the BBC Wales Film Unit. Accompanied by my new PA Myra Jervis (a tower of strength from Glasgow), I quite enjoyed the isolation.

Many documentaries emerged at this time. *Pride of Place*, a film series written by Lindsay Evans and presented by Lord Anglesey, travelled the length and breadth of Wales to feature important country houses. They were both on the Historic Buildings Council which ensured that the series would be scholarly and significant. We had great fun filming with 'Henry' (as my children called Lord Anglesey) since he had a great sense of humour and was quite an actor! *The Happiest Days* was filmed with David Parry-Jones, where we took various personalities back to their original schools: Huw Wheldon to Friars Bangor, Victor Spinetti to Monmouth School and Cliff Morgan back to the valleys of his youth. Another series, *Home Brew* with broadcaster Frank Hennessy, travelled to various pubs and featured local talent and stories, again, all over Wales. God knows how I made time for all these programmes. I am exhausted now just thinking about them!

At home, events were changing rapidly. My mother had died; Elen, our eldest, had gone to Sussex University; Siôn was specializing in music and hoping to enter Cardiff Uni's music department; and Gwenllian was growing up quickly and, horrors, was interested in a career in television. Meanwhile, I prepared for what would be my last film for the BBC. This would be *The Fasting Girl* for BBC2 – the period tale of a young girl in

Cameraman Robin, myself and Angharad James (The Fasting Girl) appreciate the Celtic Film Award.

Carmarthenshire who took to her bed and apparently fasted for months and survived. She became the object of pilgrimage until, monitored by nurses round the clock, she eventually died. This moody tale was again from the pen of Paul Ferris and required, as a main setting, a Welsh longhouse. Well, Pauline the designer and I combed the country in our search, but not one could we find. We eventually decided to re-create one behind the village of Talybont which was isolated and where we could adapt (and thatch!) two low cottages and an adjoining garage into a permanent set. Of course, when we started filming, RAF fighters would target us often with their low level bombing runs – a common problem in Wales. But we had a great cast, and eventually received the Celtic Film Award for best drama in Douarnanez, France, where I could exercise my French in the acceptance speech – critically watched by my wife (and Ken Hawkins) in the audience. This last film was actually directed by Robin Rollinson, who I had by then on trainee attachment as a director.

Only one more production of consequence remained. Shot in studio and on OB totally on video, *Sul y Blodau* (also written by Meic Povey) had Welsh and English dialogue, and examined the events one Palm Sunday when many people were rounded up by the police for questioning after a spate of 'cottage burnings'. This would also be directed by Robin and even starred the late, great Ray Gravell as a detective!

This, however, would precede a fairly fallow period in my career. I was being pressurised by management to start a new unit in Gabalfa and act as Head of Department of something to be called 'General Programmes', which would unite several current staff producers and create programmes ranging from documentaries to gardening tips. Being the 'maverick' I wasn't terribly keen on this idea. There had been pressures on me previously to join the Drama department which, in spite of numerous hot dinners and discussions, I had resisted. This time I could see that the denizens of the third floor were serious, so I approached the sage Selwyn Roderick for his advice. 'If they want you to do it, 'twere better you do it!' was his first reaction; his next was: 'You *can* do it, have faith in yourself.' Not totally convinced, I contacted the third floor (specifically Gareth Price and Teleri Bevan) and said I would accept the task for a year's trial. I little knew at that moment that this decision would limit my creative time considerably and that administrative affairs, such as planning meetings or writing annual reports, would take up so much of my time. I began to experience the frustration that Selwyn himself must have felt during all his years as departmental head.

In addition to this, two projects I had been planning for some time were cancelled by BBC London because of 'general cut-backs in programming'. These were *The Dancing Years*, a serial musical drama on Ivor Novello written by Elaine Morgan; and *Schweitzer*, about Albert Schweitzer and his life serving the poor in Lambaréné commissioned from Paul Ferris. Both were well advanced and their loss was a major blow. I had even fixed Drury Lane theatre for *The Dancing Years* and spoken to the Congolese president regarding *Schweitzer* and, of course, already had a schedule.

John Stuart Roberts by then was more involved in network projects and I assisted him by directing two of them. One was a major OB, *Gospel Rock*, starring Pat Boone and an audience of thousands in the Afan Lido, many coming by bus from Scotland! The other was an OB in Speaker's House, Parliament, entitled *Order, Order!* with George Thomas giving a St David's Day dinner to celebrity guests. Finally came *Shadowlands*, a major film for London on the life of CS Lewis starring Joss Ackland and Claire Bloom, with myself as executive producer. This last film for BBC London, shot in Cardiff and Oxford, was to win a BAFTA prize for best drama.

153

Husband and wife duo Oscar Quitak and Andrée Melly played the dithering local doctor and his sceptical wife

Two cottages and a garage near Talybont, Cardiganshire, converted by designer Pauline Harrison to look like a thatched Welsh cottage.

Author-actor Meic Povey, Leslie Duff and Ian Saynor starred in *Sul y Blodau*

Joss Ackland, in the cloisters at Oxford, stars as C S Lewis in *Shadowlands*, closely watched by my PA Myra Jervis and the rest of the crew

Back home, my father died, having contracted pneumonia after a brief period in hospital. I remember my vigil at his bedside in Cardiff Royal Infirmary and the lone street light shining through a misty gloom outside (reminding me of the wartime gas lamps in Rhondda) as he fought for breath. I could think only of the efforts he'd made in the valley, sustaining congregations, educating us and fighting for the language in the Cwm. I thought also of the two National Eisteddfod crowns he won, both in our glass cabinet at home – one for his poem on Dylan, one on the subject of my sister's death, a cathartic exercise for him. I thought then of the 'blue anemone of death' and saw it again, this time on him. Bethan, the children and I would eventually put him to rest next to my mother and sister in the grave at Llanfihangel Aberarth, overlooking the Cardigan Bay he so loved.

Back at the Beeb again, there was much talk of re-organisation of the services of television and radio. Rather than have one overall Head of Programmes, the posts of Head of TV and Head of Radio would be created. I thought nothing much about this until colleagues started coming to me saying: 'Are you trying for Head of TV?' This happened so often that I began to question myself. This called for another visit to the oracle Selwyn Roderick, who had himself been labelled a 'maverick' and been bypassed many times when top jobs were in contention. 'Go for it, *bach*,' was his reply, 'who else is there?'

I have, in fact, to this day, no idea who else was applying and never tried to find out. I told Bethan, my PA Myra and John Stuart (friend of many French and Italian summers), who also encouraged me but

157

admitted he would also be a candidate. I saw it as means of lifting me out of the present doldrums and thought I would have staff support since, over the years, I had worked with most departments and was familiar with their particular problems.

The dreaded day dawned and by 3.30pm I found myself in the Head of Admin's ante room, away from other candidates who might be departing or arriving through the foyer. Normally, on these occasions, it was 'out of the foyer and into the frying pan'. I was eventually ushered into the board room. As expected, there were the usual top brass ranged on the other side of the table: Gareth Price (Controller, Wales), Teleri Bevan (Head of Programmes, Wales), Andrew McCabe (Head of Admin.), Alwyn Roberts (Chair of the Board of Governors) and Brian Wenham (BBC2 Controller). I was relieved to see Brian because I had built up a rapport with him during his short tenure as controller; he was a possible 'network friend in the camp'. The questions ranged widely and the session lasted for one hour. Luckily, I didn't fall over the furniture on my way out. Andrew led me back to his office, saying, 'Well done!' and thanking me for attending. I couldn't get out of Broadcasting House fast enough and rushed back to Llys Aeron to be de-briefed by Bethan and to have a stiff G & T! Within 45 minutes there was a knock at the back door. It was John Stuart (his interview had been fairly brief), who also needed a large 'comforter'.

So there we sat, exchanging details regarding the interviews until 6.30pm when the phone rang. It was Gareth, thanking me for attending but eventually saying that the board had concluded that JSR was the best candidate. 'Well you'd better tell him,' I said, as I passed the receiver to John. John didn't seem surprised. I sat there and didn't know what to feel; at least I would have plenty of time to cogitate in my new cell in Gabalfa! I malingered there for some months, attending meetings, writing reports, with the occasional call from John saying that he would prefer it if I were nearer him in Broadcasting House. But the reality was that I was out of it and likely to remain so.

Then, life took a new turn when I received a call from Mervyn Williams (former Head of Music and Arts) who had left the Beeb to form his own company, Opus 3. This was staffed initially by Mervyn, Hefin Owen (former BBC Music producer) and production manager Anna Williams; hence, Opus 3. This independent company, based in Rhiwbina, made programmes commissioned by both S4C and the BBC. They were now looking to extend their portfolio by including drama – was I interested? I clutched immediately at this lifeline and arranged to meet Mervyn over a meal in one of his favoured watering holes in Birchgrove. The prospect of an early release from inactivity was too good to miss. Although I had big responsibilities at the BBC, including the National Eisteddfod coverage, I felt creatively dead.

Since the year was 1988 and I had celebrated my 50th birthday in January, I thought I might aim for early retirement. Many staff were retiring early at that time – leaving of their own volition or being pushed. I went to see Andrew, who promised to look into it. Gossip spreads like wildfire in the Beeb (well, it is in the business of communication) and all sorts of rumours were rife. I informed the 'powers that be', which by now included JSR, and said that I had made

159

up my mind: I was leaving.

Meanwhile Elen, my eldest daughter, was facing her graduate exams in Sussex University and needed support. She is now living in London, the proud mother of two delightful girls, Caitlin and Erin. As a film editor, she is the worthy recipient of a Royal Television Society Award, working on network drama and feature films like *Merlin* and *Ashes to Ashes* – even doing episodes of *Torchwood* in Wales. She is married to David Kelly, a film producer and proud London Irishman. Both her daughters are fluent Welsh speakers and destined (I think) to follow their parents into the business, in London I guess.

November '88 came, and following a short meeting with Gareth Price and Andrew McCabe (when Gareth presented me with an inscribed book of poetry by Saunders Lewis from the Gregynog Press), I walked out of Broadcasting House for the last time.

CHAPTER 7

Out on a limb?

Now that I had made the decision and was out in the cold as it were, my first worry was the maintenance of our way of life as a family. I knew that to call outside companies 'independent' was a misnomer; there is no more 'dependent' unit than a private company subject to the whim of a commissioning editor. Although I had been offered more than my previous salary, I had no yardstick to prove that I could operate in this sector of TV. Would I succeed as before? I had no real experience in handling big budgets alone, but Mervyn had no worries on this score. He ensured that I had support in this particular area by introducing me to accountant Huw Roberts and a production manager, Ian Eryri (now, sadly, passed away), who would make sure programmes were within budget. I breathed a sigh of relief. Nevertheless, I still thought I would gain more confidence if we moved house. Llys Aeron had, in a way, fulfilled its purpose. It had been a wonderful home to us and the children, then to my parents; but now my mother and father had passed away, it was time for a re-think. Elen would be leaving college, while Siôn would probably be in a hall of residence in Cardiff. Gwenllian would be the only one left, swotting for her GCE exams.

We decided that now was a good opportunity to 'downsize' and Llys Aeron was put on the market. Since we had been in Llandaff for twenty years, we searched for a three-bedroom flat in the village, which we subsequently found and remain there to this day. Coincidentally, with all this upheaval, news came of the death in a car accident of my best friend and cousin, David, from Devil's Bridge, who had been working in Denbigh for some time. We were both of the same age and his death was a tremendous blow. It led to this next poem, written after we returned from a very stormy funeral...

A CHILL WIND BLOWS

A chill wind blows today
And we are hushed,
We grapple with our memories,
Our faces flushed.

We clutch at Truth
We clutch at Life
We sway
Above the open tomb;
We are not rushed.

We pause
We contemplate,
We try
To grasp the hand
That holds the wheel;

Whose slightest twist,
Whose trick of fate,
Can launch us to
Eternity.

We can but marvel now
That saints still walk this earth;
That men will live and die
With faith sustaining them
From birth.

(RL Private poems)

It's strange how childhood memories often colour and direct our thinking even when we are adults. Meic Povey and I had been discussing various ideas for projects and we both remembered aunts or other relatives who had influenced our lives. One of mine was Megan, a spinster aunt who had been wonderfully kind to us in Devil's Bridge. She had spent all her life in service to first her parents, then a brother. This became the basis for our film drama *Nel* which became my first contribution to Opus 3 and thence to S4C. Nel was a combination of aunts Meic had known, my aunt Megan, and elements of behaviour I had seen in my mother who always cupped her hand over her mouth when laughing. It was filmed largely on location on a farm near Talyllyn with Beryl Williams as Nel, Stewart Jones as her brother Robat and a strong cast which included the young Daniel Evans who would later star in the West End. This was also to be my first collaboration with Mel Williams, the ex-BBC editor who worked in the newly established facility

Sian Phillips congratulates Beryl Williams for her performance as 'Nel', similarly I get a chance to meet my old friend Meredith Edwards as he presents me with a BAFTA award

house, Derwen, in Whitchurch. Mel would eventually edit most of my productions for S4C. This also would be my first real sortie into Welsh-language drama which would continue until my retirement.

This production was received with universal acclaim by the critics and was eventually chosen for the very first Welsh BAFTA award given for drama. I was presented the award by veteran film actor Meredith Edwards, much, I think, to the chagrin of numerous BBC bosses in the audience!

Heartened by this early success, I forged on with added confidence, knowing that there was support from Mervyn and others in areas where I was weakest. Furthermore, there was much talk in Opus of plans to expand west to Llandeilo by setting up a broadcasting centre in Newton House (known as Dynefor Castle) so that programmes more representative of this area could be based there. This led me to another series,

Y Filltir Sgwâr (The Square Mile), which, again, Meic Povey and I started discussing.

It would follow the trials and tribulations of an ex-Bangor drama lecturer (to be played by Dyfed Thomas) who decides to move to the wilds of Carmarthenshire and begin a new career writing for television! Whilst I was working up this project, I also did a documentary for Mervyn on *Côr y Bont*, the Pontarddulais male choir, but this did not distract me from my ultimate aim of cornering the market in Welsh-language drama.

Eventually *Y Filltir Sgwâr* was ready to go and, after a short location shoot in Bangor Uni, we settled into a corner of the Towy Valley which would be our home for some months. We had an old farmhouse which had a tidemark halfway up its walls; fortunately (I'm pretty lucky with weather) it didn't rain for the *entire* filming period. The Towy was at its most idyllic; so were the artistes and crew. Here I started a good working relationship with cameraman Alwyn Roberts who had a facilities studio called 'Enfys' in Cardiff. He would be cameraman on many of my productions. One particular surprise for me was the number of ex-colleagues and BBC-trained staff who had opted for the freelance life. Of course, there are many who have arrived from other sources of training. Although the BBC has a remit to include a percentage of 'independent' productions, I, for one, never worked again to their commission. All my dramas were a direct result of an S4C commission. Many came from a good relationship that I had with Dafydd Huw, in charge of S4Cs drama output. During these projects, not once did I feel that my 'independence' was being challenged by either Opus or Dafydd in S4C.

Y Filltir Sgwâr crew at Plas Dinefwr, Llandeilo

By the time it came for us to edit *Y Filltir Sgwâr* Opus had moved into the castle in Llandeilo, to which I daily made the one and a half hour journey from Cardiff. The journey was pleasant and the company and Mel at the other end were welcoming. The opening in Llandeilo was in the form of a party given to important guests of the broadcasting establishment who were then shown around the new facilities. All seemed set fair for a long and prosperous future in Llandeilo, but then, circumstances have a habit of changing.

Unaware of any possible threat to our future there, I pressed on with preparing the next project to be set in west Wales; this would be another contemporary drama series set on and around a ferry in Fishguard. Meic would also write this. Several visits to the Stena Line HQ in Goodwick terminal secured their cooperation and, when possible, free passage and facilities relating to the ferry operation in Fishguard and the crossing to Rosslare. This series, entitled *Halen yn y Gwaed* (Salt in the Blood), would have Dafydd Hywel, Stewart Jones, Nicola Beddoe and Sue Jones-Davies as the main characters and a large cast of stalwart supporting Welsh players, including William Thomas and Phil Harries providing regular comedy relief. One thing I had not realised when crewing this was that cameraman Alwyn Roberts was seasick and loathed the open sea – in fact was quite green when in harbour. Helicopters and planes he managed without a qualm, but the briny was to be avoided! He never mentioned or complained about this, which was a tribute to his professionalism. I, on the other hand (coming from a family of seafarers), was sick on buses.

So for me and my crew it became 'life on the ocean waves' for some months until we eventually edited the series on dry land – in Derwen, Whitchurch. During this time, drama producer Gwyn Hughes Jones (an ex-BBC colleague) also entered the frame. He had decided to leave the Beeb and try the independent game. He would eventually help me by directing episodes of this series.

Another *divertissement* occurred at this time when I was asked to assist with a challenge to the ITV franchise in Wales. Confidential, it involved many high-powered 'names' and required considerable finance for the bid. I don't intend listing these names here (I hear sighs of relief all round) but I was co-opted as a prospective Head of Welsh Programmes should the bid succeed. Mervyn let me take time off for this; a period which would involve me in drafting potential programme plans, visiting venture bankers in London and secretly

Halen yn y Gwaed

securing potential staff members. The bid was thick and substantial but unfortunately the IBA decided to continue with the previous holders – HTV. There is, you will gather, material for another book here, but that is for someone else to write. I was glad to return to the real business of TV production.

The resultant series was nominated for a Welsh BAFTA but was pipped at the post by a BBC Wales production.

It became clear eventually that for Opus (now Opus 30) there was competition looming from other independent companies where S4C commissions and money were concerned. One company had chosen

Llanelli as its base and would eventually move ahead in the race. In the interim, I had prepared another project with Meic Povey, again to do with extremist activity. *Y Weithred* (The Deed) portrayed the activities of three young Welshmen who led a campaign against the drowning of Capel Celyn village to form Tryweryn reservoir. This would end up being my last major stand-alone project for television. *Y Weithred* would not actually be on film but, in the fashion of the day, on digital widescreen video, shot as on film with single camera. Again the cameraman would be Alwyn and the designer John Thompson (a humorous and able artist, originally from Port Talbot, who became a great friend) with a strong crew led by Derwyn Williams, the production manager. The action would require the recreation of explosions which happened in various locations, particularly the site of the construction camp building the dam. For this we needed to build our own credible site which we did in a remote valley behind Llanuwchllyn, with huts, bulldozers and cranes in evidence.

Electronic inlay was used considerably to marry into our images those of the long-gone village and the dam itself. Powerful performances of the three principal characters were achieved by actors Robin Eiddior (as Owain Williams), Julian Lewis Jones (as John Albert Jones) and Jeremi Cockram (as Emyr Llew). I will always remember the anticipation of a huge crowd of local on-lookers who gathered one night on the bare mountainsides to watch the pyrotechnics as we recreated the explosions. This was a very moving and emotive piece of Welsh television; I even received a letter from Norah Isaac, then in poor health, who said, 'Thank

Y Weithred: Robin, Jeremy and Julian with mock-up of construction camp in background

you for lifting the standard of television in Wales,' and, 'I was embarrassed to belong to a generation which had sat by while Wales was being despoiled.' This was generally the reaction among viewers and we were satisfied that we had somehow captured the mood and motives for this 'extremist' act.

In the heat (or explosion) of this activity, Opus 30 had decided to relinquish the castle to the National Trust and to return to Cardiff where they are still based. Gwyn Hughes Jones completed a production I had prepared called *Yr Ynys*, an imaginary tale of a Welsh-speaking commune which had set up on an off-shore island in Pembrokeshire to maintain their language and customs. My knowledge of that coast was particularly useful when choosing locations. With the performances of John Ogwen, JO Roberts and others, Gwyn made a very powerful statement here.

Opus 30 continued to expand its staff, with my son Siôn eventually joining as a trainee. He had done a B.Mus. in Cardiff but was keen to get a grounding in television. I realise this could smack of nepotism, but I had little to do with it, or him for that matter. Doctors' sons tend to become doctors, artists' sons become artists, and on it goes. Think of the Dimbleby family – all in the same game. All three of my children have made their careers in the media of their own volition; in fact, my experiences should have had the reverse influence. As I mentioned before, Elen is a film editor, Siôn directs music and drama, Gwenllian (now mother of two – Macsen and Lleu) produces a well-known soap. My wife Bethan is permanently in a state of pique because not one has wanted to become a French teacher. Although, fair play, Siôn is currently studying a language – Spanish!

My last TV production was an epic saga recounting the history of a Cardiganshire family setting up the milk trade in London. *Y Palmant Aur* (The Golden

Admiring the John Thompson model of the snowy London features in *Y Palmant Aur*

Pavement) would follow members of the family through three generations; in other words, three series! Written by Manon Rhys (daughter of firebrand Kitchener Davies), whose own family came from Llwyncelyn and Aberaeron, it would require a large cast and period settings, wardrobe and props. It eventually spawned a series of novels by Manon based on the series. Since some of the action would take place in period London streets, we decided to build sets in an old wartime hanger in Llandow near Cowbridge which designer John Thompson tackled with relish. Other locations like Harley Street we shot in Newport. The country locations were shot on the actual sites: Aberaeron, Llwyncelyn and New Quay; my old holiday haunts.

By this time, another drama person had been appointed to Opus. This was Eryl Huw Phillips, an actor who had caught the directing bug! Thank God, because after the first series, he and Gwyn would have to take over.

I had been conscious for some time that (unsurprisingly) my blood pressure was creeping up. I knew this because, as freelancers, we had to have regular medical MOTs in order for us to be properly insured. As men do, I had tended to ignore these signals, in spite of Dr Cann Jones (my old neighbour who carried out insurance checks) having kindly drawn my attention to the condition. It all came to a head one day when on my way to Opus (early as usual) with nobody around, I suffered a massive nosebleed which I had difficulty in stopping. I went home and eventually found the courage to tell the wife, who immediately rang our doctor and made an appointment. Dr Wheeler in Fairwater, who had treated our family for years, sat me down and took a reading. Now he was a fairly cool, undemonstrative type and 'tut-tutted' audibly. I think I blew the top off his machine. He called for a second opinion; he also stared in disbelief!

'How did you get here?' Wheeler asked.

'Er, I drove,' was my limp reply.

'Well,' said the good doctor, 'you'd better drive home very slowly and get your wife to take you to Llandough A&E department. I'll arrange things.'

I managed to get Bethan out of class and she drove apprehensively to the hospital. Once there, I was whisked into a bed with nitroglycerine placed under my tongue and wires attached to every available part of my body. Suddenly, the young doctor in charge said, 'Don't I know you?' As it transpired he was the son of my other neighbour, Dr Keith Young, when we lived in St Michael's Road. So from then on, I was 'Uncle Dic'. Yes, I was lucky to be alive, the nosebleed being a timely warning. Thereafter, I spent a week in bed, largely ignored, whilst I received numerous scans and medication which brought my pressure down to reasonable levels. As somebody who had only ever had trivial health problems (like hay fever), this was a traumatic and salutary experience.

The conclusion was obvious: if you want a life (if you want to live!) then at a certain age you must change your lifestyle, stop working and start relaxing. Having come through this experience unscathed (except mentally you might say), I immediately told Mervyn that I was retiring as soon as convenient. Sensibly, under his direction, I had taken out a private pension to supplement my BBC pension and this would provide

me and the family with a fairly comfortable retirement. Our flat in Nice and the move to our apartment in Llandaff seemed to make a lot of sense now. Within a few months I had persuaded Bethan to join me; she retired from Ysgol Glantaf. We both adopted a lifestyle which I called 'the complete and absolute avoidance of stress' – trying to eat sensibly at regular times and not taking on any duties that would aggravate my condition. My blood pressure is now, I'm pleased to say, at very acceptable levels. As they say: 'Keep taking the tablets!'

Today, eleven years on, we are content, travelling every two months to Nice to soak up the Mediterranean sun and more often to London or Penylan to babysit. I occasionally watch television, carefully pre-selected and, preferably, pre-recorded. I have come to the conclusion that television is very much a creature of its time and even the best archives tend to lie forgotten

Gwenllian, Siôn and Elen at the National Eisteddfod, 2008 in Cardiff

Erin and Caitlin in London

Macsen and Lleu in Penylan

in dusty vaults; many recorded on, by now, unplayable formats. At least good art can hang on public view in galleries or on somebody's wall, often appreciating in value with the passage of years. This is not to say that I am disenchanted with the medium – in particular film – and I certainly enjoyed every moment of my working life. However, I now think that my best productions were, in fact, our children!

On my 70th birthday, I was moved to receive a bound copy of my photographs together with accompanying DVD from the children, which, in part, was the impetus for me to write these notes.

To paraphrase a saying: 'There's no business like *family* business!'